Eyewitness
Titanic

T.S.S. TITANIC

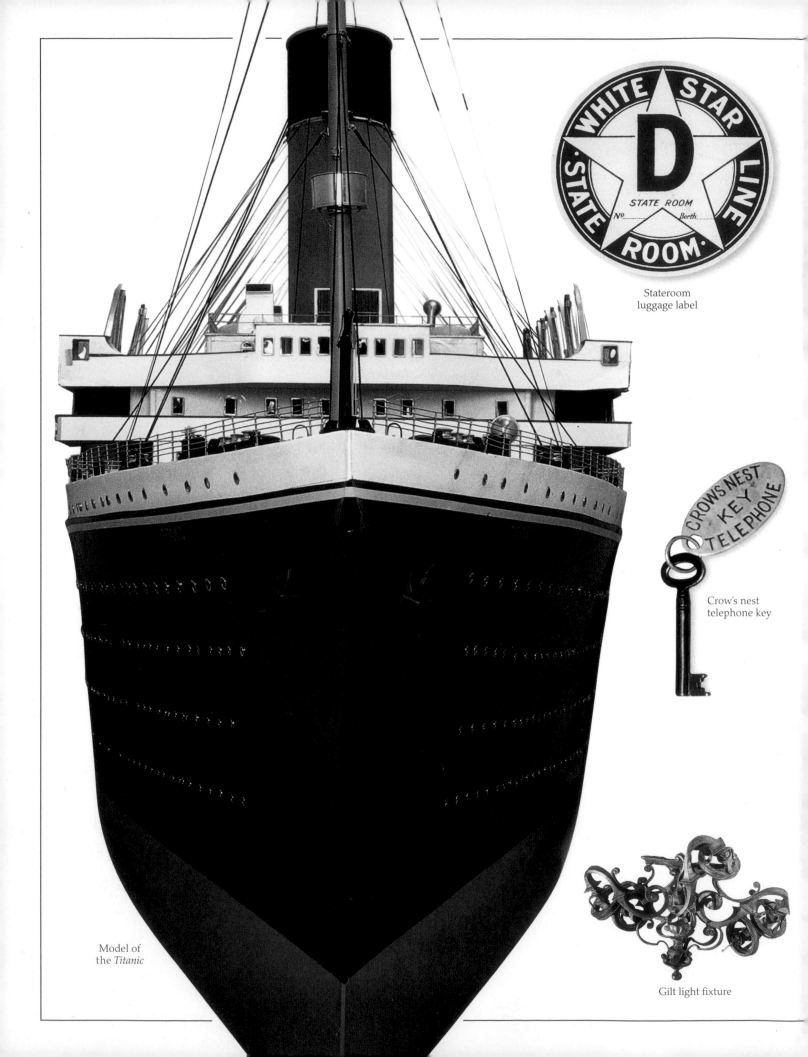

WHITE STAR LINE

D

STATE ROOM·

STATE ROOM

Nᵒ   Berth

Stateroom
luggage label

CROWS NEST
KEY
TELEPHONE

Crow's nest
telephone key

Model of
the *Titanic*

Gilt light fixture

First-class bathtub faucets

Eyewitness
Titanic

Written by
SIMON ADAMS

Bell from crow's nest

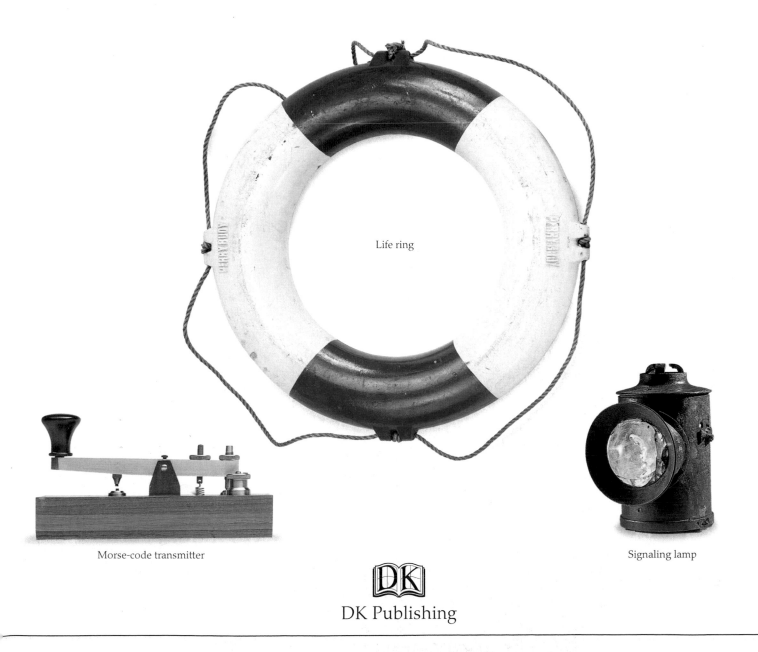

Life ring

Morse-code transmitter

Signaling lamp

DK
DK Publishing

Compass head

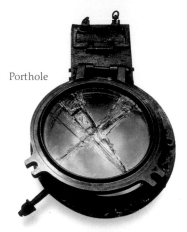

Porthole

Logometer

LONDON, NEW YORK,
MELBOURNE, MUNICH, AND DELHI

Project editor Melanie Halton
Art editor Mark Regardsoe
Designer Polly Appleton
Senior managing editor Linda Martin
Senior managing art editor Julia Harris
Production Kate Oliver
Picture researcher Claire Taylor
DTP Designer Andrew O'Brien

REVISED EDITIONS
Consultants Ted Turner, Simon Adams
Editorial Kitty Blount, Sarah Phillips, Jayne Miller
Design Andrew Nash, Edward Kinsey
Managing editor Camilla Hallinan
Managing art editors Jane Thomas, Owen Peyton Jones
Art director Martin Wilson
Associate publisher Andrew Macintyre
Production editors Jenny Jacoby, Siu Yin Ho, Laragh Kedwell
Production controllers Jen Lockwood, Pip Tinsley
Picture research Bridget Tilly, Deborah Pownall, Myriam Megharbi
U.S. editorial Elizabeth Hester, Beth Sutinis
U.S. design and DTP Dirk Kaufman, Milos Orlovic
U.S. production Chris Avgherinos

Memorial badge

This Eyewitness ® Guide has been conceived by
Dorling Kindersley Limited and Editions Gallimard

First published in the United States in 1999
This revised edition published in 2004, 2009
by DK Publishing, 375 Hudson Street,
New York, New York, 10014

A catalog record for this book is available from the Library of Congress.
ISBN 978-0-7566-5036-0 (HC); 978-0-7566-0733-3 (ALB)

Color reproduction by Colourscan, Singapore
Printed by Toppan Co., (Shenzhen) Ltd., China

Discover more at
www.dk.com

Compass stand

Captain Smith

Contents

White Star Line
playing cards

Overseas travel

RED STAR LINE
One of the many lines that ran steamships across the Atlantic, the Red Star Line of Belgium was bought by John Pierpont Morgan in 1902 and became part of the International Mercantile Marine Company, which also owned the White Star Line, soon to build the *Titanic*.

IN THE DAYS OF SAIL, ships took weeks, if not months, to travel between continents, and passengers were as likely to die from disease as they were to be shipwrecked or drowned. The development of large, fast, and relatively safe steamships during the mid-1800s transformed travel by sea, allowing people to cross the ocean faster and more cheaply than ever before. Shipyards built bigger and faster passenger ships—now called liners, after the shipping lines they were built for—and furnished them in great luxury to attract high-paying, first-class passengers. It was into this competitive world that the *Titanic* was launched.

Statue of Liberty overlooks New York Harbor

LIBERTY BECKONS
For many steerage (third-class) passengers on board the North Atlantic liners, theirs was a one-way journey, away from the poverty and oppression of Europe to start a new life in the "New World"—the Americas. Between 1900 and 1914, more than 12 million people immigrated in this way. By 1914, one-third of the United States' total population of 92 million was made up of immigrants.

SIRIUS
The first steamship to cross the Atlantic entirely under steam power was the *Sirius*, a 783-ton (711-metric ton) paddle steamer built in Glasgow, Scotland, in 1836. The *Sirius* left London on March 28, 1838, for Queenstown, Ireland, where it took on 40 passengers and 503 tons (457 metric tons) of coal. It arrived in New York on April 22 after an eventful 18-day crossing, during which the crew was forced to burn cabin furniture and the emergency mast when the ship ran short of coal.

Mast to take sails if engine failed

Hull measured 207 ft (63 m)

Paddle wheels driven by steam engine

GREAT EASTERN
Five times larger than any existing ship, the *Great Eastern* was designed by Isambard Kingdom Brunel (1806–1859), the greatest engineer of his time. Carrying 13,440 tons (12,193 metric tons) of coal, the ship could take 4,000 passengers all the way to Australia without refueling. But passengers refused to travel in such a large vessel and, in 1863, three years after its maiden voyage, the *Great Eastern* became a cable-laying ship.

Six masts carried 58,501 sq ft (5,435 sq m) of sail

Great Eastern was 682 ft (208 m) long, 118 ft (36 m) wide, and weighed 21,186 tons (19,220 metric tons)

Each paddle wheel was 57 ft (17.5 m) in diameter

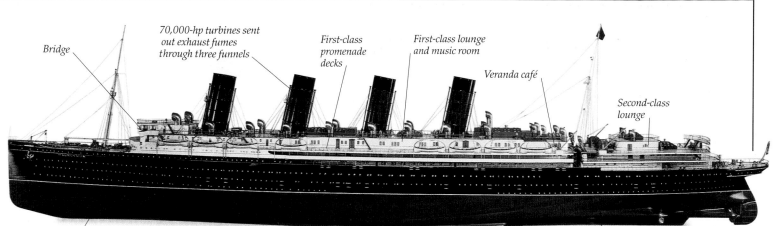

Bridge

70,000-hp turbines sent out exhaust fumes through three funnels

First-class promenade decks

First-class lounge and music room

Veranda café

Second-class lounge

Observation room

MAURETANIA

Along with its sister ship, the *Lusitania*, the *Mauretania* was the pride of the Cunard Line (below left). The *Mauretania* was equipped with four giant steam turbines, a revolutionary new engine capable of generating 75 percent more power than the equivalent engine used in the *Titanic*. As a result, on its maiden voyage in 1907, the *Mauretania* set a new speed record for crossing the Atlantic—four days and 19 hours, at an average speed of 27.4 knots (31.5 mph/50.7 kph)—a record unchallenged until 1929.

The Mauretania *was 748 ft (228 m) long and weighed 35,000 tons (32,000 metric tons)*

Ornate marble pillars

THE WHITE STAR LINE
Founded in 1871 by Liverpool shipowner Thomas Ismay, the White Star Line grew from a bankrupt fleet of clipper ships operating between Britain and Australia. The Belfast shipyard Harland and Wolff won the contract to build every new White Star ship.

THE CUNARD LINE
Samuel Cunard ran a successful shipping business in Halifax, Nova Scotia, in Canada, with his brother Joseph before establishing a shipping line to carry mail from England to Canada in 1839. The Cunard Line soon established itself as the major North Atlantic shipping line, and a direct rival to White Star.

"Everything has been done in regard to the furniture and fittings to make the first-class accommodation more than equal to that provided in the finest hotels on shore."

EXTRACT FROM *THE SHIPBUILDER*

LUXURY LINERS
No expense was spared in decorating the Atlantic liners. For first-class passengers, the public rooms and staterooms (cabins) were furnished in a variety of styles drawn from history, often emulating great country houses in their lavish use of hardwoods, marble, and gilt. For second-class passengers, the rooms were more than adequately furnished, while many third-class passengers encountered good sanitation and table linen for the first time in their lives.

SHIPPING TYCOON
The US banker, industrialist, steel magnate, and railroad owner John Pierpont Morgan was one of the richest men of his era. In 1902 he bought up a number of European shipping lines to create a vast and prosperous shipping firm— the International Mercantile Marine Company—that dominated shipping across the North Atlantic Ocean.

Building the *Titanic*

Ever since its foundation in 1871, the White Star Line had ordered its new ships from the shipyard of Harland and Wolff in Belfast, Northern Ireland. The design and construction skills of the yard were outstanding, and the workforce took great pride in the many famous ships they built. Construction of the *Titanic* began on March 31, 1909, and work progressed at a furious speed from then on. Every day, the yard reverberated to the sound of heavy machinery and incessant hammering. First the keel plates were positioned. Then, once the framework was in place, the beams and deck plates were installed and the steel hull plates, some of them 30 ft (9 m) long, were fixed together by more than 3 million rivets. By May 1911, less than two years after work began, the *Titanic* was ready to be launched.

THRIVING WORKFORCE
The usual workforce of Harland and Wolff, which numbered about 6,000 people, more than doubled in size to cope with the construction and fitting out of both the *Titanic* and its sister ship, the *Olympic*. The shipbuilder was the biggest single employer in Belfast, and its workforce lived in the maze of narrow streets surrounding the dockyard.

SHIPPING ENTREPRENEUR
Lord William Pirrie, chairman of the Belfast shipyard Harland and Wolff, had worked for the company since 1862. In 1907, Lord Pirrie and Bruce Ismay, chairman of the White Star Line, devised a plan to build three magnificent liners. With the emphasis on luxury and safety, the liners were to transform transatlantic travel.

"a waste of money…
she's too big… she'll
bump into summat…
no ship's unsinkable…"

SIR J. BISSET

UNDER CONSTRUCTION
The first of the new White Star liners to be built was the *Olympic* (far right), with the *Titanic* (left) following a few months later. The liners were so big that special slipways had to be built to accommodate them. Above the slipways was a vast gantry carrying a central revolving crane and 16 movable cranes.

*Anchor weighed 17 tons
(15.75 metric tons)*

GIANT ANCHOR
The *Titanic*'s enormous central anchor was the biggest of the ship's three anchors. It took a team of 20 horses to haul the heavy load to the shipyard, ready for installation on the forecastle (bow) deck. The two side anchors were half the weight of the central anchor. The side anchors were raised and lowered by 107 tons (97.5 metric tons) of cable.

IN DRY DOCK
After its launch on May 31, 1911, the *Titanic* was pulled by tugs into the dry dock, where work began on equipping the empty hull. Engines, boilers, and other pieces of machinery were installed; cabins, staterooms, and dining areas were built and equipped to accommodate passengers. On February 3, 1912, the *Titanic* was moved to the dry dock (below), where propellers were added and a final coat of paint was applied.

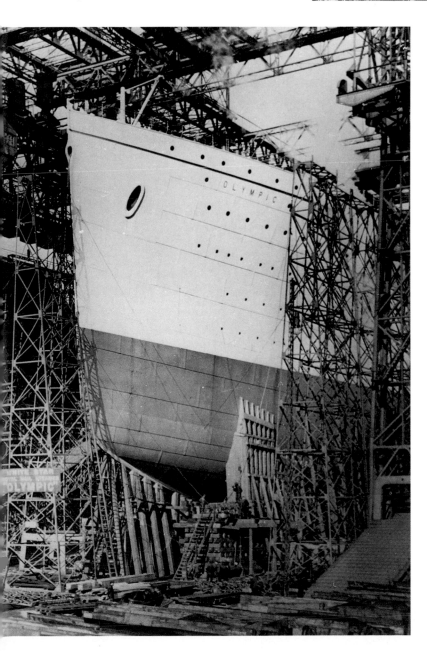

The central propeller shaft awaits the addition of its huge bronze propeller

DRIVING FORCE
Three massive turbine shafts connected the engines to the propellers at the rear of the ship. Two of these shafts drove the outer propellers, which each consisted of three bronze blades bolted into a steel hub. The central shaft (above) drove the forward-only, four-bladed propeller.

CAST IN BRONZE
The two outer propellers each measured 23 ft 5 in (7 m) in diameter, while the smaller, central propeller was 16 ft 5 in (5 m). Because its blades were made of bronze, the starboard, or right, propeller (above) remained well-preserved on the seabed after the ship sank.

Fast and "unsinkable"?

DESPITE POPULAR BELIEF, the *Titanic's* designers never claimed the ship was unsinkable or exceptionally fast. The ship was designed for luxury and comfort rather than speed, and was actually about 4 knots (4 mph/7 kph) slower than its Cunard rivals. The *Titanic's* builders, Harland and Wolff, claimed that the ship's system of watertight bulkheads "made the vessel virtually unsinkable." The word "virtually" was soon forgotten, however, as the sheer size and solidity of the *Titanic*, together with its grandeur and opulence, encouraged most people to believe that the ship truly was unsinkable.

Massive A-frame supports engine

Shipyard worker dwarfed by colossal engine

MIGHTY ENGINES
The *Titanic* was driven by two massive reciprocating steam engines, which powered the ship's two outer propellers. At more than 30 ft (9 m) tall, the reciprocating engines were the largest ever to have been built at that time. Steam from these two monsters passed into a 470-ton (427-metric ton), low-pressure turbine engine and traveled along the turbine shaft, providing the power to drive the forward-only center propeller.

LETTING OFF STEAM
Each reciprocating engine had four huge cylinders through which steam passed to drive the propeller shafts. So well built were the engines that some of the cylinders survived, almost intact, long after the ship sank.

Some boilers weighed more than 100 tons

GIANT BOILERS
Down in the depths of the ship's hull, 29 boilers, containing 159 furnaces, powered the engines. Together, the furnaces consumed 728 tons (660 metric tons) of coal a day and produced 46,000 horsepower, driving the ship at a top speed of about 23 knots (26 mph/42 kph). Here, the boilers are seen lined up in Harland and Wolff's boiler shop prior to installation.

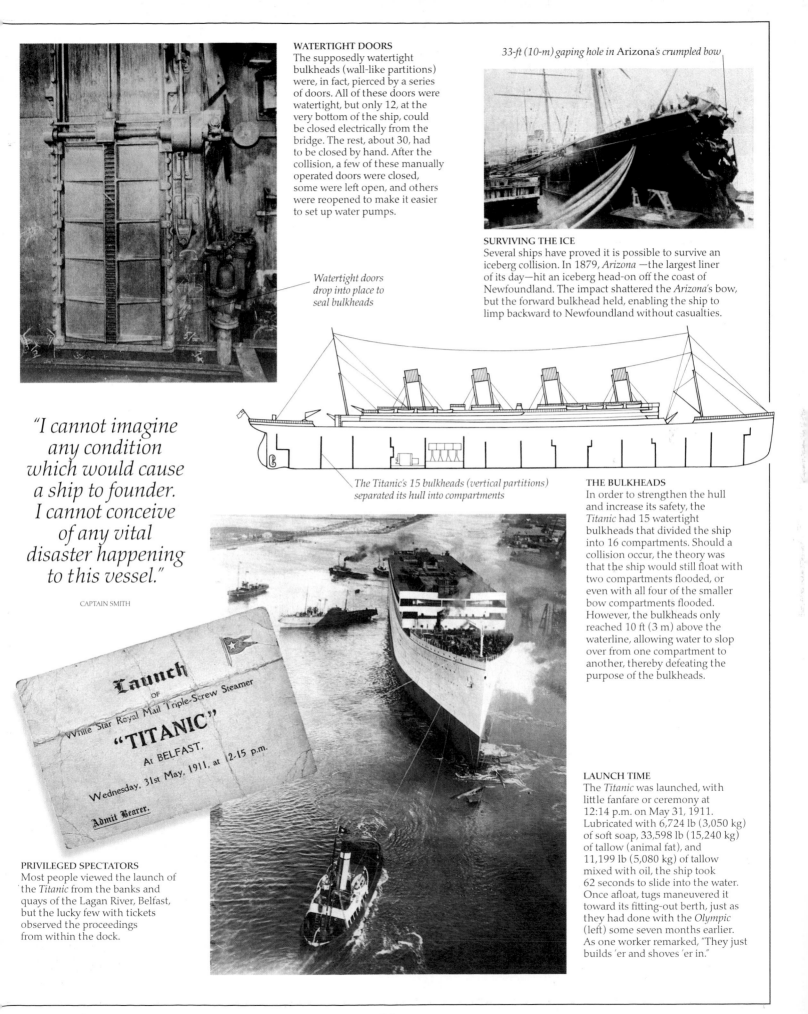

WATERTIGHT DOORS
The supposedly watertight bulkheads (wall-like partitions) were, in fact, pierced by a series of doors. All of these doors were watertight, but only 12, at the very bottom of the ship, could be closed electrically from the bridge. The rest, about 30, had to be closed by hand. After the collision, a few of these manually operated doors were closed, some were left open, and others were reopened to make it easier to set up water pumps.

33-ft (10-m) gaping hole in Arizona's crumpled bow

SURVIVING THE ICE
Several ships have proved it is possible to survive an iceberg collision. In 1879, *Arizona*—the largest liner of its day—hit an iceberg head-on off the coast of Newfoundland. The impact shattered the *Arizona's* bow, but the forward bulkhead held, enabling the ship to limp backward to Newfoundland without casualties.

Watertight doors drop into place to seal bulkheads

"I cannot imagine any condition which would cause a ship to founder. I cannot conceive of any vital disaster happening to this vessel."

CAPTAIN SMITH

The Titanic's 15 bulkheads (vertical partitions) separated its hull into compartments

THE BULKHEADS
In order to strengthen the hull and increase its safety, the *Titanic* had 15 watertight bulkheads that divided the ship into 16 compartments. Should a collision occur, the theory was that the ship would still float with two compartments flooded, or even with all four of the smaller bow compartments flooded. However, the bulkheads only reached 10 ft (3 m) above the waterline, allowing water to slop over from one compartment to another, thereby defeating the purpose of the bulkheads.

Launch
OF
White Star Royal Mail Triple-Screw Steamer
"TITANIC"
At BELFAST,
Wednesday, 31st May, 1911, at 12-15 p.m.
Admit Bearer.

PRIVILEGED SPECTATORS
Most people viewed the launch of the *Titanic* from the banks and quays of the Lagan River, Belfast, but the lucky few with tickets observed the proceedings from within the dock.

LAUNCH TIME
The *Titanic* was launched, with little fanfare or ceremony at 12:14 p.m. on May 31, 1911. Lubricated with 6,724 lb (3,050 kg) of soft soap, 33,598 lb (15,240 kg) of tallow (animal fat), and 11,199 lb (5,080 kg) of tallow mixed with oil, the ship took 62 seconds to slide into the water. Once afloat, tugs maneuvered it toward its fitting-out berth, just as they had done with the *Olympic* (left) some seven months earlier. As one worker remarked, "They just builds 'er and shoves 'er in."

RMS *Titanic*

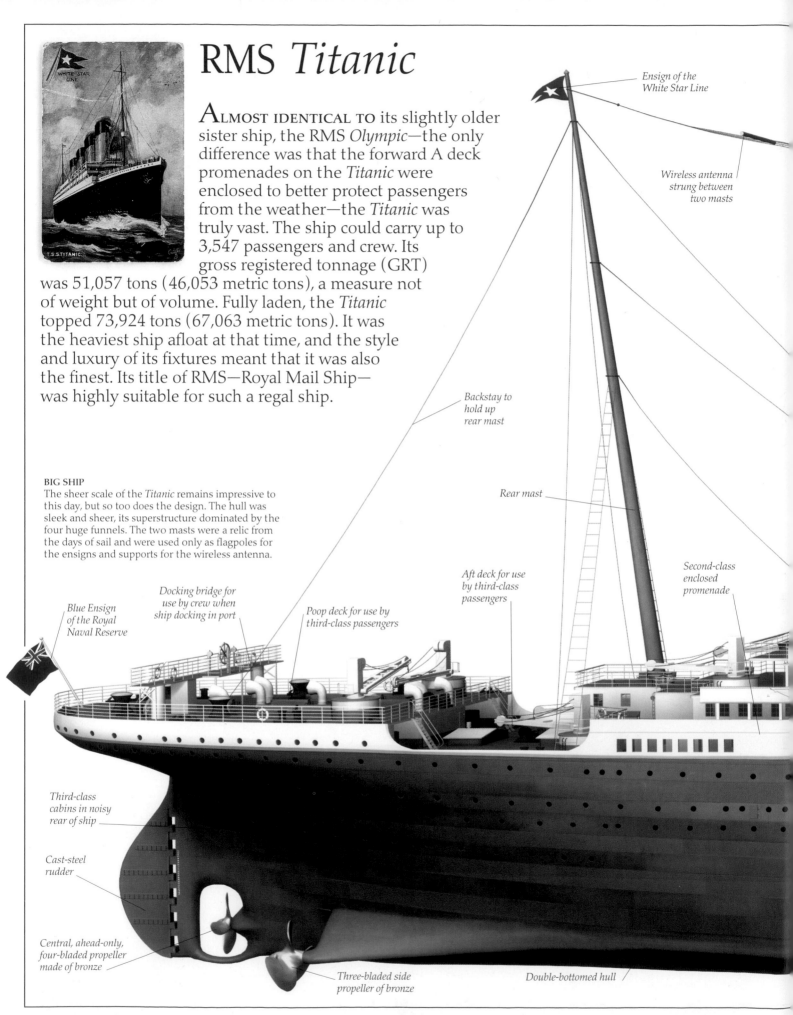

ALMOST IDENTICAL TO its slightly older sister ship, the RMS *Olympic*—the only difference was that the forward A deck promenades on the *Titanic* were enclosed to better protect passengers from the weather—the *Titanic* was truly vast. The ship could carry up to 3,547 passengers and crew. Its gross registered tonnage (GRT) was 51,057 tons (46,053 metric tons), a measure not of weight but of volume. Fully laden, the *Titanic* topped 73,924 tons (67,063 metric tons). It was the heaviest ship afloat at that time, and the style and luxury of its fixtures meant that it was also the finest. Its title of RMS—Royal Mail Ship— was highly suitable for such a regal ship.

BIG SHIP
The sheer scale of the *Titanic* remains impressive to this day, but so too does the design. The hull was sleek and sheer, its superstructure dominated by the four huge funnels. The two masts were a relic from the days of sail and were used only as flagpoles for the ensigns and supports for the wireless antenna.

Ensign of the White Star Line

Wireless antenna strung between two masts

Backstay to hold up rear mast

Rear mast

Aft deck for use by third-class passengers

Second-class enclosed promenade

Docking bridge for use by crew when ship docking in port

Poop deck for use by third-class passengers

Blue Ensign of the Royal Naval Reserve

Third-class cabins in noisy rear of ship

Cast-steel rudder

Central, ahead-only, four-bladed propeller made of bronze

Three-bladed side propeller of bronze

Double-bottomed hull

HOW LONG?
If you placed 22 double-decker buses end to end on the deck of the *Titanic*, they would stretch from the ensign mast at the stern to the forestay fitting at the bow—a total of 883 ft (269 m).

BREATH OF FRESH AIR
The boat decks provided plenty of space for passengers to stretch their legs and enjoy the sea air. Deckchairs—shown here stacked up ready for use—were available for those wishing to sit and relax, although the lifeboats hanging from their davits restricted the view of the sea.

"Perhaps the most striking features… are the four giant funnels—huge tawny brown and black capped elliptical cylinders of steel which tower 175 ft (53 m) from the keel plate, dominating the other shipping in the port, and dwarfing into insignificance the sheds on the quayside."

EXTRACT FROM THE *SOUTHAMPTON PICTORIAL*

Rear ventilation funnel

Glass dome covering first-class stairway leading down to first-class smoking room and cafés

First-class staterooms

A deck open promenade for first-class passengers

Second-class entrance to boat deck

Continued on next page

On the bridge

The nerve center of the *Titanic* was the bridge, which was situated at the front of the boat deck. From this viewpoint the captain and his senior officers commanded the ship, surveying the sea in front of them and issuing orders to the engine room. Although the ship was steered from the wheelhouse, the captain had a small auxiliary wheel on the bridge that he could use in case of emergencies.

PORTHOLES
The sides of the ship were lined with portholes from the first-class suites on C deck down to the third-class berths on the lower deck. The portholes allowed light and fresh air into the cabins. At night, cabin lights shone out through the portholes, sparkling along the length of the dark hull.

"Like the Olympic, yes, but so much more elaborate. Take the dining saloon—Olympic didn't even have a carpet, but the Titanic—ah, you sank in it up to your knees."

BAKER REGINALD BURGESS

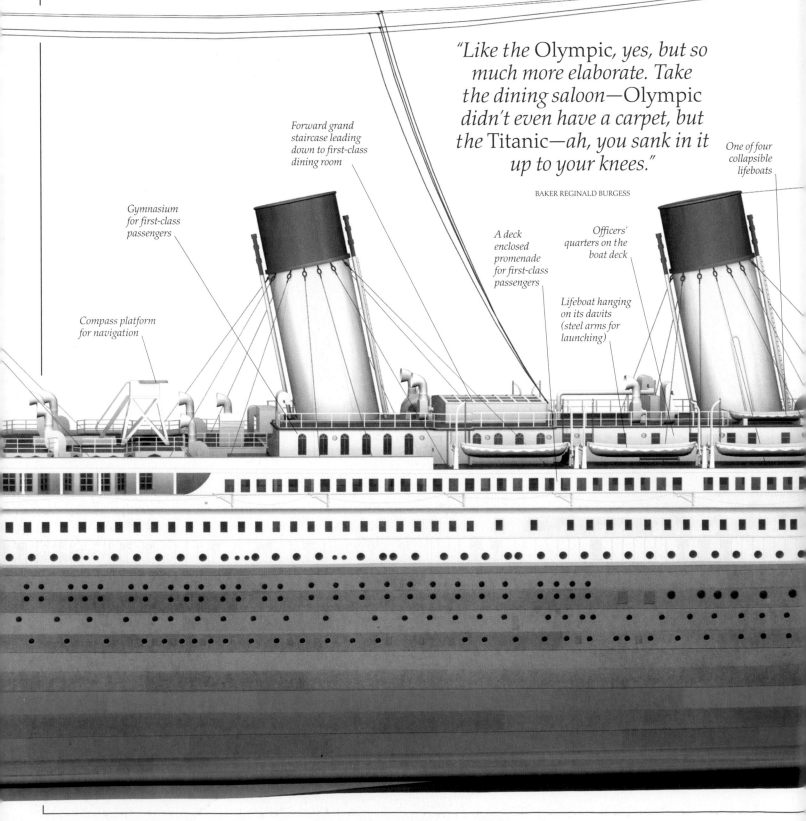

Gymnasium for first-class passengers

Compass platform for navigation

Forward grand staircase leading down to first-class dining room

A deck enclosed promenade for first-class passengers

Officers' quarters on the boat deck

Lifeboat hanging on its davits (steel arms for launching)

One of four collapsible lifeboats

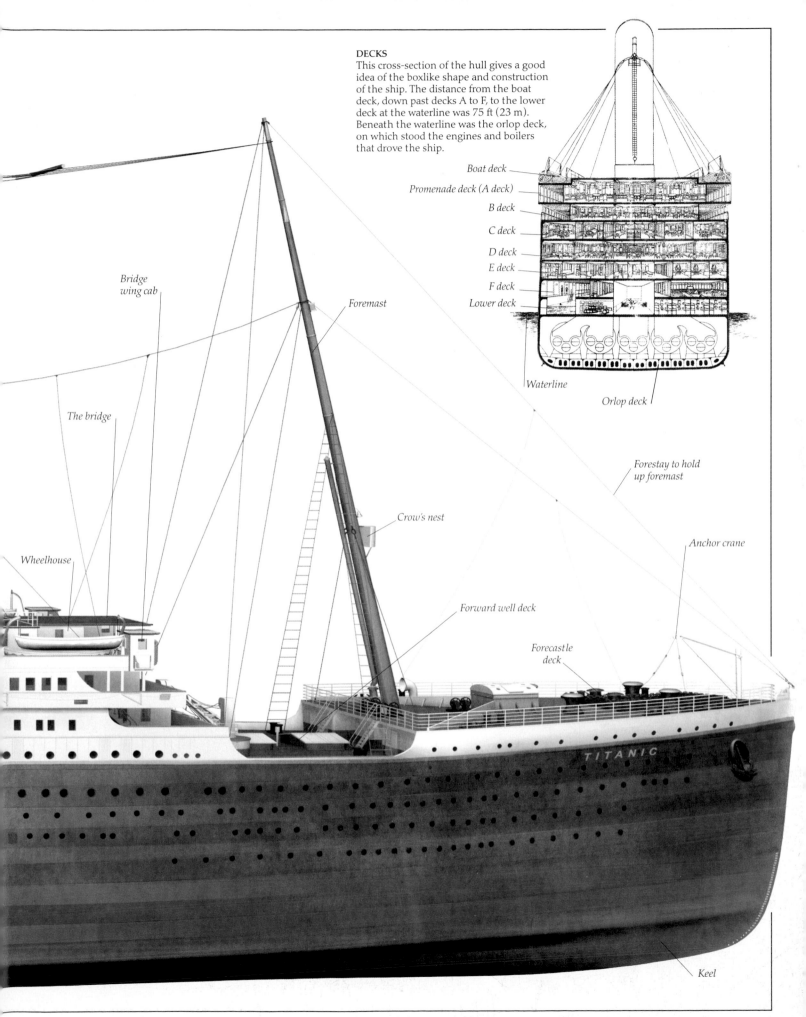

DECKS
This cross-section of the hull gives a good idea of the boxlike shape and construction of the ship. The distance from the boat deck, down past decks A to F, to the lower deck at the waterline was 75 ft (23 m). Beneath the waterline was the orlop deck, on which stood the engines and boilers that drove the ship.

Boat deck

Promenade deck (A deck)

B deck

C deck

D deck

E deck

F deck

Lower deck

Waterline

Orlop deck

Bridge wing cab

Foremast

The bridge

Forestay to hold up foremast

Crow's nest

Wheelhouse

Anchor crane

Forward well deck

Forecastle deck

TITANIC

Keel

Fine fixtures

PROUD TO SUPPLY
The *Titanic* was so prestigious that suppliers were proud to announce they supplied the ship with certain goods. The message in this advertisement was clear: you too can share in some of the *Titanic*'s luxury, even if you cannot afford to sail on it.

IN ITS DRY DOCK in Belfast, Northern Ireland, the *Titanic* was transformed from an empty hull into a fully equipped floating palace in little more than eight months. No expense was spared in making the *Titanic* the most luxurious liner afloat. Close attention was paid to every single detail—from the design of the large public rooms and open decks to the individual light fixtures and faucets in the cabins. Everything on board was bought brand-new or specially made for the ship; and everything was designed to make the passengers comfortable and to entertain them during the voyage.

WASHED UP
Some of the thousands of white dishes on board ship survived the crash, remaining in neat rows just as they were originally stacked. An army of crew members filled these dishes with food and served meals to the passengers.

Gold-plated and crystal light fixtures lit up each landing of the grand staircase

Painter adds highlights to features on a decorative column

Rails of wrought iron and gilt bronze

FINISHING TOUCHES
Some indication of the care and attention to detail taken in equipping the *Titanic* can be seen in this photograph of plasterers and decorators at work on its sister ship, the *Olympic*. Period detail was lovingly recreated by expert craftsmen in the many first-class rooms and cabins.

Ornate columns of polished oak

Late 17th-century-style cherub lamp support

GRAND STAIRCASE
Leading from the first-class dining room on D deck up to the first-class promenade deck, the grand staircase was one of the most stunning features on board. The staircase was lit from above by natural light through a wrought iron and glass dome and illuminated at night by gold-plated crystal lights. First-class passengers, dressed in all their finery, swept down the staircase on their way to dinner.

ON TAP

Every cabin or suite had running water, a luxury few of the third-class passengers would have enjoyed at home. However, there were only two bathtubs for the 700 third-class passengers. Located at the very back of D deck, it was a long walk for those sleeping in the bow.

First-class bath faucets recovered from the Titanic wreck site

ON THE VERANDA

One of the most popular rooms on board, especially among the younger passengers, was the veranda café. The café was light and airy with white wicker furniture, a checkered floor, and ivy growing up trellises on the walls.

READING ROOM

The white-paneled reading room was a favorite retreat for women, who were forbidden to join the men in the smoking room. With its comfortable chairs and plentiful space, the reading room was the ideal place to write a letter or read a book, a selection of which was available from the ship's large library.

Clock surrounded by two figures symbolizing Honor and Glory crowning Time

Gilt light fixture crumpled in wreck

LIGHT FANTASTIC

The light fixtures in the first-class lounge matched the Louis XVI style of the room. Elsewhere, crystal chandeliers and ceiling lights glittered over the assembled passengers.

UPLIFTING

Located just forward of the grand staircase, three elevators took first-class passengers from the promenade deck down five decks to their cabins, passing the staterooms, the dining room, and other cabins on their way. The elevators were magnificently decorated and well-disguised behind classical pillars. One elevator near the stern of the ship served second-class passengers.

Captain and crew

Hidden from view was a vast army of workers, whose job it was to keep the passengers fed and well looked after, and the ship cleaned, properly equipped, and efficiently powered. Chefs, bakers, butchers, scullions (kitchen workers), mailroom staff, barbers, engineers, firemen, stokers, trimmers (luggage loaders), and many others slaved away on the lower decks. Up on the public decks, stewards, pursers, waiters, and other uniformed crew tended to passengers' needs. In total, there were 898 crew members, including the captain and his senior officers, who were responsible for every aspect of life aboard the ship.

THE STOKERS
Working in shifts, the 289 firemen and stokers shoveled coal into the boilers to keep the engines working at full speed. Many of the workers sang as they worked to keep their spirits up.

THE POWER HOUSES
Located deep in the bowels of the ship, the boiler rooms were hot, noisy, and dirty. A team of 28 engineers ensured that all ran smoothly; for if the boilers ran out of coal or stopped working, the ship would grind to a halt.

Chief Purser Herbert McElroy *Second Officer Charles Lightoller* *Third Officer Herbert Pitman* *Fourth Officer Joseph Boxhall* *Fifth Officer Harold Lowe*

Sixth Officer James Moody

THE OFFICERS
The captain and his officers are seen here on board the *Titanic* prior to its maiden voyage. The captain wore naval medals won during the Boer War (1899–1902). Stripes on the sleeves of officers' uniforms show an individual's rank—the more stripes, the more senior the officer.

Chief Officer Henry Wilde *Captain Edward Smith* *First Officer William Murdoch*

SAM COLLINS
While on board the *Carpathia*, fireman Sam Collins (above) befriended the young Frankie Goldsmith, whose father went down with the *Titanic*. Frankie had been fascinated by the firemen on the *Titanic* and had watched them at work in the engine rooms.

Loading mail sacks onto the Titanic

MAIL SHIP
The *Titanic* had a contract with the British Royal Mail to carry mail across the Atlantic. The mail was stored in the hold with the first-class luggage and sorted in a room next to the squash court. The five clerks working in the hold were among the first to notice water pouring in through the hull.

Pocket watch stopped at 2:16 a.m.; the ship finally sank at 2:20 a.m.

Rusty penknives

Propelling pencil

RECOVERED LIFE
First-class steward Edmond J. Stone was responsible for staterooms E1 to E42. His body was one of the first to be recovered by the *Mackay-Bennett*, and he was buried at sea. Stone's personal effects (left), which were returned to his widow, included part of a letter from the P&O Steam Navigation Company dated February 2, 1912. Stone was evidently trying to gain employment with one of White Star's main rivals.

AT YOUR SERVICE
The first-class à la carte restaurant was run by Monsieur Gatti, the owner of an exclusive French restaurant in London. Gatti's team of 55 cooks and waiters were all French or Italian and, since they were not employed by White Star, had no status on board the *Titanic*. The restaurant staff suffered greatly when the ship went down; only one survived.

"The night before sailing I asked my wife to put my white star in my cap, and while she was doing it the star fell all to pieces. With a look of dismay, she said, I don't like this."

STEWARD ARTHUR LEWIS

Violet Jessop

Annie Robinson

Some of the surviving stewardesses pictured on their arrival in Plymouth, England.

THE STEWARDESSES
Out of a crew of 898, there were only 18 stewardesses. Despite the mix of sexes among the passengers, the old superstition about women at sea—and the social attitudes toward women at that time—dictated White Star Lines' employment policies. But the "women and children first into the lifeboats" rule ensured that 17 of the stewardesses survived the disaster.

Children's toys hang from the ceiling

Souvenir pennants

Reclining chair

SHOP AND SHAVE
Two barber shops—one in first class, the other in second—offered men a daily hot lather and shave. The shops also sold toys, postcards, and other souvenirs of the voyage, such as paperweights and commemorative plates.

ON RECORD
Fireman William Nutbeam was one of only 35 out of the 167 firemen to survive the voyage. His Continuous Certificate of Discharge (logbook) is marked "vessel lost" against the *Titanic* entry. Other entries in the book include the *Olympic* and the *Oceanic*.

Predicting the tragedy

THERE ARE MANY STRANGE STORIES relating to the *Titanic*. Some are so bizarre that few people believe them. Others are tales of prediction and foreboding that uncannily described the real-life events of the *Titanic* disaster. Two authors came close to describing the events of that fateful night, some 20 years before they actually occurred. A number of people had recurring dreams of the forthcoming disaster, and a dying girl in Scotland related the events of the night just hours before they unfolded. Numerous people had such strong premonitions of disaster that they refused to board the *Titanic*. For all those people who deliberately avoided traveling on the ship, however, some were simply very lucky and failed to board on time.

COLLISION VISIONS
New York lawyer Isaac Frauenthal had a dream before boarding the *Titanic*. "It seemed to me that I was on a big steamship that suddenly crashed into something and began to go down." He had the dream again when on board the *Titanic*, and so was alert to the danger when he first heard about the iceberg collision. Unlike other passengers, Frauenthal needed no encouragement to board a lifeboat.

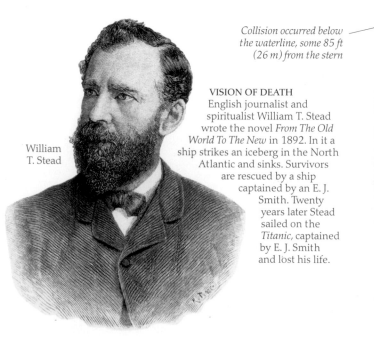

William T. Stead

Collision occurred below the waterline, some 85 ft (26 m) from the stern

VISION OF DEATH
English journalist and spiritualist William T. Stead wrote the novel *From The Old World To The New* in 1892. In it a ship strikes an iceberg in the North Atlantic and sinks. Survivors are rescued by a ship captained by an E. J. Smith. Twenty years later Stead sailed on the *Titanic*, captained by E. J. Smith and lost his life.

A BAD OMEN
An ominous warning of the forthcoming tragedy occurred on September 20, 1911, when the *Titanic's* sister ship, the *Olympic*, collided with the warship HMS *Hawke*. Both ships were badly damaged, and the *Olympic*, under Edward J. Smith, soon to captain the *Titanic*, was found to be at fault.

> *"That ship is going to sink before it reaches America."*
>
> MRS. BLANCHE MARSHALL

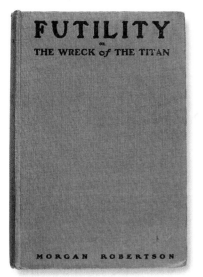

FUTILITY

In 1898, a retired merchant navy officer, Morgan Robertson, wrote a novel called *Futility or The Wreck of the Titan*. The book's description of a ship attempting to cross the Atlantic in record time, hitting an iceberg, and sinking with the loss of almost all of its passengers due to a shortage of lifeboats, predicts the fate of the *Titanic* almost faultlessly.

JESSIE'S DREAM

On the night of April 14, 1912, a young Scottish girl, Jessie, was being comforted as she lay dying. In her delirious state Jessie had a vision of a ship sinking in the Atlantic. She saw many people drowning and "someone called Wally… playing a fiddle." Within hours of her death, the *Titanic* slowly sank as Wally Hartley and the rest of the band continued to play.

Ceramic figurine coated with turquoise glaze (around 700 BCE)

LUCK OF THE PHARAOHS

As first-class passenger Molly Brown left her cabin, she grabbed the Egyptian statuette that she carried with her for good luck. It stayed with her until she was rescued by the *Carpathia*, when she presented it to Captain Rostron as a thank-you present.

Reverend J. Stuart Holden's unused Titanic ticket

LUCKY ESCAPE

Among the 55 passengers who canceled their bookings at the last moment was John Pierpont Morgan, owner of the White Star Line and hence of the *Titanic* itself. Steel baron Henry Frick and railroad owner George Vanderbilt, both from the United States, were two others who decided not to sail. Reverend J. Stuart Holden of London escaped the disaster because his wife became ill.

MISSING THE BOAT

Many crew members were recruited by word of mouth in the pubs of Southampton, England. Twenty-two recruits failed to board the ship in time, notably the three Slade brothers, who were prevented from reaching the ship by a long goods train passing through the docks. One recruit reached the quayside and then, filled with a sense of foreboding, decided against boarding the ship.

Interior of the Belvedere Arms, one of the many pubs in Southampton where people were recruited for work on board the Titanic

HISTORY REPEATS

In April 1935, the *Titanian*, a tramp steamer carrying coal from Newcastle, England, to Canada, encountered an iceberg in the same area as the *Titanic* had done 23 years earlier. Crew member William Reeves had a premonition seconds before the iceberg came into view and yelled "Danger ahead!" to the navigator, who quickly reversed the engines and brought the ship to a halt. Reeves was even born on April 15, 1912—the same date on which the *Titanic* sank.

Maiden voyage

SOUTH WESTERN HOTEL
A number of the wealthier passengers spent the night before the voyage in the South Western Hotel, Southampton, overlooking *Titanic*'s dock. Among those who enjoyed the hotel's luxury was Bruce Ismay, chairman of the White Star Line, and his family.

THE FIRST VOYAGE OF A NEW SHIP—its maiden voyage—is always an important occasion, and the *Titanic*'s was no exception. The ship arrived in Southampton, England, on April 3, 1912, after an overnight voyage from Belfast, Northern Ireland. For the next week, the dockside bustled with activity as the crew was enlisted, and the mountain of supplies needed for the voyage was loaded on board. At last, the great day arrived, and on the morning of April 10, 1912, passengers boarded the ship. At noon, the ship slipped its moorings and began to pick up speed. The maiden voyage had begun.

Strong locks to keep contents secure during voyage

High-quality luggage was an essential fashion accessory among wealthy passengers.

SEA TRIAL
The first voyage of the *Titanic* was a short series of sea trials in Belfast Lough, on April 2, 1912. During the trials the engines were tested, the ship was maneuvered at different speeds, and an emergency stop was conducted, bringing the ship to a halt in about half a mile (1 km) after traveling at 20 knots (22 mph/37 kph). The ship left that evening for Southampton and began its maiden voyage eight days later.

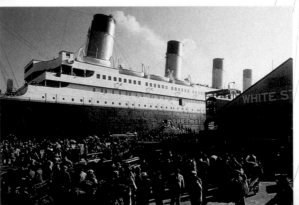

ALL ABOARD
On the morning of the *Titanic*'s departure, crowds gathered to wave goodbye to friends and relatives. Cries of, "Good luck *Titanic*," resounded as the ship slipped its moorings and set off on its first, and final, journey.

White Star Line's Southampton pier teems with life on the morning before the Titanic *departs*

Rear funnel was for show only, so it never actually belched out smoke

Tugs escort the Titanic *out of its dock to begin sea trials*

CHANNEL HOPPING

The *Titanic*'s route took the ship across the English Channel to Cherbourg, France, where more passengers boarded. During the night, the ship recrossed the Channel to Queenstown (now Cobh), Ireland. On the afternoon of April 11, the *Titanic* finally left Europe behind and set off across the North Atlantic for New York.

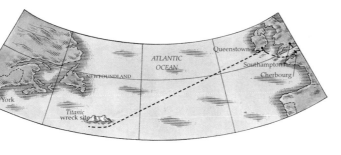

FAREWELL TO EUROPE

The *Titanic* made a brief stop at Queenstown, Ireland, anchoring offshore to pick up seven second-class and 113 steerage (third-class) passengers and more bags of mail. Many of the steerage passengers were leaving Ireland to start a new life in the United States.

The New York *narrowly escapes crashing into the* Titanic

"The ship is so big that I have not yet found my way about. I hope I shan't get lost on board before I arrive in New York!"

A PASSENGER

A NEAR MISS

As tugs maneuvered the *Titanic* out of its dock, the ship began to pick up speed as it passed the moored *New York*. Wash from the *Titanic*'s engines caused the *New York* to break free of its moorings and swing out in front of the *Titanic*. Quick action by the tugs averted a collision, but it was an ominous start to the maiden voyage.

First-class travel

THE ASTORS
With a personal wealth estimated at $87 million (£18 million) in 1912, Colonel John Jacob Astor IV was the wealthiest passenger on board. Recently divorced, the 46-year-old was returning to New York with his 18-year-old second wife, Madeleine, after their honeymoon in Egypt and Paris. Also traveling with them was their Airedale dog, Kitty.

W**ITH MOST OF THE TOP** four decks reserved for their use only, the 329 first-class passengers sailed in lavish comfort. The luxury they enjoyed on land was duplicated on board, with each stateroom, cabin, public lounge, and dining room furnished to the highest and most opulent standards. A vast workforce of personal servants, stewards, bakers, cooks, and waiters catered to the passengers' every whim. When not resting in their cabins, first-class travelers had the use of a gymnasium, a squash court, a swimming pool, a Turkish bath, a library, and a range of dining rooms, bars, and restaurants, as well as unlimited access to fresh air on the top decks.

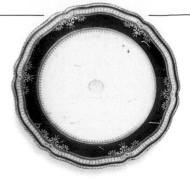

AT THEIR SERVICE
Other than elegant plates, the first-class diners had use of 1,500 champagne glasses, 400 asparagus tongs, 100 pairs of grape scissors, 1,000 finger bowls, and 300 sets of nutcrackers.

R.M.S. "TITANIC

APRIL 14, 1912.

LUNCHEON.

CONSOMMÉ FERMIER   COCKIE LEEKIE
FILLETS OF BRILL
EGG À L'ARGENTEUIL
CHICKEN À LA MARYLAND
CORNED BEEF, VEGETABLES, DUMPLINGS
FROM THE GRILL.
GRILLED MUTTON CHOPS
MASHED, FRIED & BAKED JACKET POTATOES

CUSTARD PUDDING
APPLE MERINGUE   PASTRY
BUFFET.
SALMON MAYONNAISE   POTTED SHRIMPS
NORWEGIAN ANCHOVIES   SOUSED HERRINGS
PLAIN & SMOKED SARDINES
ROAST BEEF
ROUND OF SPICED BEEF
VEAL & HAM PIE
VIRGINIA & CUMBERLAND HAM
BOLOGNA SAUSAGE   BRAWN
GALANTINE OF CHICKEN
CORNED OX TONGUE
LETTUCE   BEETROOT   TOMATOES
CHEESE.
CHESHIRE, STILTON, GORGONZOLA, EDAM,
CAMEMBERT, ROQUEFORT, ST. IVEL.
CHEDDAR

Iced draught Munich Lager Beer 3d. & 6d. a Tankard.

À LA CARTE
This menu for the last luncheon served on board the *Titanic* shows the generous choice of dishes on offer. The first-class dining room had seating for more than 550 people, and recessed bays allowed small parties to dine in privacy.

Starched white linen napkins and tablecloths

Tables decorated with fresh flowers and baskets of fruit

DINNER AND DANCE
The seven-course evening meal was the social highlight of the day. Women wore their finest new gowns from Paris; the men wore evening suits. After the meal, the more energetic passengers took to the dance floor, although dancing was not allowed on Sundays. Other men retired to the smoking rooms and women to the various lounges. Passengers who had overindulged could retire to the comfort of their cabins.

LUGGAGE LABELS

Every item of luggage was carefully labeled, either for delivery to the cabin or to be stored in the hold until disembarkation. The correct sorting of luggage was particularly important among first-class passengers since they often carried large quantities of belongings. Mrs. Charlotte Cardoza and her son, for example, traveled with 14 trunks, four suitcases, three crates, and a medicine chest.

IN STATE

The first-class staterooms (private cabins) were lavishly decorated and very spacious, particularly the two promenade suites on B deck. At a cost of $4,246 (£870) in 1912, the occupants of these staterooms had the use of a sitting room, two bedrooms, two dressing rooms, and a private bathroom, as well as a private deck for enjoying the sea air.

Writing desk

French Empire-style chairs and table

"My pretty little cabin with its electric heater and pink curtains delighted me… its beautiful lace quilt, and pink cushions, and photographs all round… it all looked so homey."

LADY DUFF GORDON

The mechanical camel was especially popular

KEEP FIT

The gymnasium—situated off the boat deck on the starboard (right) side of the ship—was fully equipped with rowing and cycling machines, weights, and other equipment to keep the first-class passengers in good shape.

Silver service provided by waiters

TURKISH DELIGHT

A Moorish fantasy of enameled tiles, gilded decorations, and shaded bronze lamps, the Turkish baths contained hot, temperate, and cool rooms, a shampooing room, and a massage couch, as well as a plunge pool in which to cool off. The baths, like the gymnasium, had separate sessions for men and women.

Second-class travel

DINING IN STYLE
This dinner plate—one of 12,000 carried by the *Titanic*—from the second-class service demonstrates the strict class structure on board. Each class ate from a different style of plate.

ON BOARD THE *TITANIC*, second class was anything but second rate, for the facilities far surpassed those of first-class facilities in most rival liners. The dining room was paneled in oak and provided a four-course dinner followed by nuts, fruit, cheese, cookies, and coffee. When not dining, passengers could make use of the sycamore-paneled library, a range of bars and lounges, and, for men, the barber's shop. The cabins were comfortable and compact, and the open decks provided space for recreation and relaxation. For second-class passengers, life on board was first rate.

A NERVOUS PASSENGER?
Many passengers took the opportunity of the brief stop at Queenstown, on April 11, to mail letters to friends and relatives, telling them about life on board. Perhaps the writer of this letter was a nervous passenger since they report, "we have been having very rough weather," although the overnight passage across the Channel was, in fact, very calm.

On board R·M·S·"TITANIC."
April 11. 1912

Dear Mother & all at Home. I am now taking the opportunity of sending you a few lines about how we started from Southhampton. The Express Train quickly brought us from Waterloo. Ettie saw me off at that Place. We have been having very rough weather.

FATHER AND DAUGHTER
Alongside the rich and famous were many passengers whose lives would ordinarily have been remembered only by family and friends. Second-class passengers Robert Phillips and his daughter, Alice, embarked at Southampton: Alice survived, her father died, but their photographs ensure their immortality as two people caught up in an extraordinary event.

Passengers dwarfed by huge funnels

ON DECK
The boat deck had plenty of space for passengers to take a stroll or relax in deckchairs; children could run around and play games. A safer ship would have had less room, however, since much of the deck space would have been filled with extra lifeboats.

Traveling rug to keep out the cold

WHITE STAR LINE
SOUTHAMPTON-CHERBOURG-NEW YORK
★ SECOND CLASS ★

M
Passenger to
Per R.M.S.   Sailing
NOT WANTED
TRAINS MET ON ARRIVAL AT SOUTHAMPTON

IN THE HOLD
Those passengers heading for a new life in the Americas did not need all of their luggage during the voyage and so stored most of it in the hold. Second-class passengers may not have had as much luggage as those in first class, but they would all have traveled with evening wear for dinner and other special events.

Second-class label for luggage to be stored in the hold

THE HART FAMILY
Benjamin Hart, a builder from Essex, England, was immigrating to Winnipeg, Canada, with his wife, Esther, and his seven-year-old daughter, Eva. Esther thought the idea of the *Titanic* being "unsinkable" was "flying in the face of God," and tried to persuade her husband to change ships. Convinced that disaster would overcome them all, she slept during the day and kept watch at night. Eva and her mother survived the tragedy, but, sadly, her father was lost.

"No effort had been spared to give even second-cabin passengers… the best dinner that money could buy."

A PASSENGER

BUNKED UP
Although not as luxurious as first-class accommodation, the 207 second-class cabins were more than comfortable. Located on D, E, F, and G decks, the cabins were equipped with mahogany furniture and slept two to four passengers in single beds or bunks.

Basin for washing and shaving

Wooden seat

Iron legs

White Star Line playing cards

GAMES OF RISK
Playing cards was an ideal way to while away the time during a long voyage. But those who chose to gamble took a risk; professional cardsharps, traveling under assumed names, hoped to collect big winnings from unsuspecting players.

IN A SPIN
In the dining room, passengers sat on swivel chairs attached to the floor, a style of seating common in first-class dining rooms aboard most other liners of the time. Although the food was prepared in the same galley as the first-class meals, the second-class menu was simpler, but no less filling.

Third-class travel

DURABLE MATCHES
Using every excuse to promote its name, the White Star Line sold boxes of matches bearing the company logo. This box was recovered—unusable, but still recognizable—from the seabed.

MORE THAN HALF OF THE TOTAL 1,324 passengers on the *Titanic*—710 in all—were traveling steerage (third class). This truly international collection of people came from all over Europe and were on their way to start a new life in America. More than 100 of the third-class passengers were Irish and had left their troubled island from the emigrants' traditional departure point of Queenstown. Many had never been to sea before, few had any belongings, and all were leaving Europe with mixed feelings—regret for the homes and loved ones they were leaving behind, and nervous anticipation for the new world that awaited them. On board, 220 cabins housed families, while single people were separated: women in cabins at the rear, men in a large dormitory in the bow.

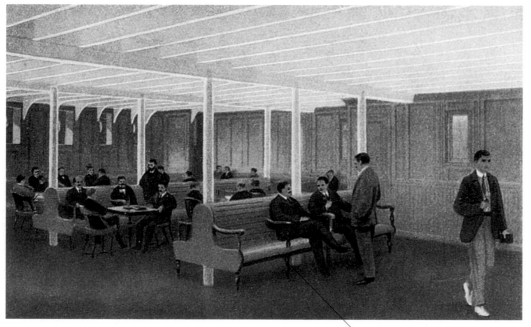

"We were emigrants, my parents had a public house in London… we were going to Kansas, my father was going to buy a tobacconist's shop."

MILLVINA DEAN

Durable benches of slatted teak

THE GENERAL ROOMS
Paneled with pine and furnished with sturdy benches, tables, and chairs, the general room—the third-class equivalent of a lounge—and the smoking room were the only public rooms available to third-class passengers. Here they chatted, read, played games, and smoked. In the evenings they entertained themselves with singing and dancing.

Leather satchel recovered from the wreck site and restored

LIFE IN A BAG
Unlike those in first and second class, most passengers in third class traveled light, having only a few valuables and personal belongings.

OPEN DECK
Buffeted by the wind and blasted by smoke from the ship's funnels, the rear decks allocated to third-class passengers nevertheless provided a welcome respite from the crowded cabins and dining rooms below. As the *Titanic* left Queenstown on April 11, Eugene Daly stood on the rear deck and played *Erin's Lament* on his Irish bagpipes, a poignant farewell to his homeland.

SHIFT WORK
In order to feed everyone in the dining room, which had space for only 473 people, third-class passengers ate in shifts. They were each given a ticket indicating which sitting they were to attend. Passengers who missed their sitting went hungry.

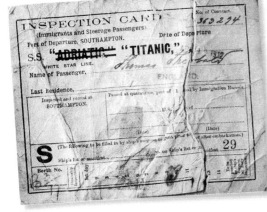

INSPECTION CARD
Each emigrant was issued with a green inspection card stating place of departure (Southampton, Cherbourg, or Queenstown) and the holder's last country of residence. This simple document was designed to help the immigration authorities in New York. Thomas Theobald's inspection card (left) shows that he was transferred from the *Adriatic* to the *Titanic*—a move that cost him his life.

Dining saloon

Four-berth cabin

THE GOODWIN FAMILY
Like many other large families, Frederick and Augusta Goodwin and their six children, including baby Sidney (not shown here), were emigrating from London to America. The Goodwins reached the boat deck too late to board a lifeboat, and all were lost.

TWO MONTHS TO PAY
This advertisement for the voyage that never happened—the return of the *Titanic* to England—gives a good idea as to the cost of a third-class ticket. At $36.25 (£7.46), the price was equivalent to about two months' wages for most third-class passengers.

Atlantic crossing

TITANIC ILLUMINATIONS
At night, the *Titanic* shone from end to end as cabin lights burned and upper decks were lit up for those wishing to walk in the night air.

As THE *TITANIC* SPED across the North Atlantic on Sunday April 14, 1912, it picked up a series of messages from other ships in the area, warning about ice. Captain Smith was firm in his belief that his ship was in no danger and was urged on by Bruce Ismay, the ship's owner, to prove the vessel's speed and reliability by getting to New York earlier than expected. "Full speed ahead," remained the instruction, and although the captain steered the ship 16 miles (25.7 km) to the south before turning toward New York, no other notice was taken of the increasingly detailed reports about the ice ahead.

Two clocks to show the time at the ship's location and at its destination

WIRELESS ROOM
The use of wireless on board ship was still a novelty at the time of the *Titanic*'s maiden voyage. Radio operators spent their time dealing with personal messages and did not need to be on 24-hour duty. Until the *Titanic* disaster, few people realized the importance of radio as a form of emergency communication.

Battery charging panel

Magnetic detector, or "Maggie"

10" spark transmitter

Headphones for hearing incoming messages

Morse-code keys for sending messages

Telegraph message pad

Transmitter tuning coil

Fleming valve tuner

Marconi telegraph codes book

Multiple tuner for receiving Morse-code signals

Wireless operator's logbook

MARCONI WIRELESS OPERATORS
The *Titanic*'s two wireless operators, Jack Phillips and Harold Bride (left), were employed by Marconi rather than the White Star Line. Second Wireless Operator Bride was only 22 years old and had worked for Marconi for less than a year. He was paid about $25 (£12.50) a month to work the night shift while his senior colleague, Phillips, rested.

TO FRIENDS AND FAMILY
Although the majority of passengers communicated with friends and family by sending letters and postcards, many wealthy passengers took advantage of the *Titanic*'s ship-to-shore telegraph to transmit personal messages. The workload was so heavy that First Wireless Operator Phillips interrupted the final ice warning from the *Californian* in order to continue transmitting.

> *"Captain, Titanic—Westbound steamers report bergs, growlers, and field ice in 42ºN from 49º to 51ºW, April 12."*
>
> TELEGRAPH FROM CAPTAIN BARR OF THE *CARONIA*

WARNING MESSAGE

As the *Titanic* steamed westward toward the ice, it received nine messages—by telegraph and signal lamp—warning of the danger ahead. Although not all of these ice warnings reached the bridge, the message from the German steamer *Amerika* (above), sent about four hours before the *Titanic* hit the iceberg, was passed to Captain Smith in person.

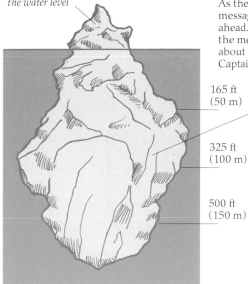

Only 10 percent of an iceberg is visible above the water level

165 ft (50 m)

Beneath the sea's surface, an iceberg is bulky, with many sharp edges capable of puncturing a ship's hull

325 ft (100 m)

500 ft (150 m)

HIDDEN DANGER

It is difficult to gauge the real size of an iceberg because 90 percent of its bulk is hidden beneath the sea. Icebergs are formed when chunks of freshwater ice break away from glaciers and float into the sea. There, the chunks are broken up by ocean tides, currents, and waves. Icebergs can be up to 150 miles (240 km) long and 70 miles (110 km) wide, although smaller "growlers" and floating drift ice are also common.

Icebergs can tower above the sea like mountains, or lie flat on the water like frozen fields

BRUCE ISMAY

As chairman of the White Star Line, Bruce Ismay was in the odd position of being a passenger on board a ship he owned. It was Ismay's influence that caused Captain Smith to accelerate through the icefield rather than slow down or stop for the night.

JOURNEY OF AN ICEBERG

The icebergs of the North Atlantic begin life in the glaciers of the polar icecap and are carried south by the icy currents of the Labrador Sea, between Canada and Greenland. Except during a few short summer months, icebergs are found well to the south of Newfoundland, Canada. Some are so large that they survive at sea for several years before melting in warmer waters.

A deadly collision

THE NIGHT OF APRIL 14, 1912, was clear and bitterly cold on the North Atlantic Ocean. There was no Moon, but the cloudless sky was full of stars. The sea was glassy calm, giving no indication of the danger lurking ahead. As a routine precaution, the lookout men up in the crow's nest were warned to watch out for icebergs. Because it was such a clear night everyone thought there would be plenty of time to avoid any obstacles in the sea. But large ships at full speed do not turn quickly or easily, and when lookout Fredrick Fleet spotted an iceberg, at about 11:40 p.m., it was too late to avoid a collision. The *Titanic* struck the iceberg.

Warning bell is 17 in (43 cm) in diameter

Mast light indicated the ship's direction of travel

EMERGENCY BELL
As the iceberg loomed into view, Fleet struck the crow's-nest bell three times—the accepted signal for danger ahead. At the same time, he telephoned the bridge to tell them what he saw.

FRED FLEET
Frederick Fleet, one of six lookouts on board the *Titanic*, was on watch in the crow's nest, high up on the foremast. At about 11:40 p.m. he saw what he thought was a small iceberg, directly ahead. As the ship approached, he realized that the iceberg was considerably bigger than he originally thought. Quickly, he hit the warning bell.

CROW'S-NEST KEYS
Not all the crew who sailed the *Titanic* down from Belfast were hired for the ship's maiden voyage. David Blair was one of the unlucky ones, and in his rush to pack and leave the ship, he came ashore with the keys to the crow's nest telephone in his pocket.

Hatch through which lookouts entered and left the crow's nest

FALLEN FOREMAST
Although severely damaged, the crow's nest is clearly visible on the fallen foremast. From this vantage point, two lookouts kept watch around the clock for icebergs, ships, and other hazards.

On board, few of the passengers felt anything more than a slight judder

Open section of bridge from which Murdoch observed the iceberg, seconds after the warning from the lookout

Covered wheelhouse in center of bridge

"It was as though we went over about a thousand marbles."

MRS. STUART J. WHITE, PASSENGER

ON THE BRIDGE
Although the bridge is the command headquarters of a ship, only four officers were on the *Titanic's* bridge at the moment of impact. One other officer had just gone into the officers' quarters, and Captain Smith was in his cabin, next to the wheelhouse. As three of these six officers subsequently lost their lives in the tragedy, it remains unclear exactly what happened in the vital seconds before and after the collision.

TOWER OF ICE
The *Titanic* struck the iceberg a glancing blow on the starboard (right) side of its hull and the damage appeared only slight. According to eyewitness accounts, the iceberg towered up to 100 ft (30 m) over the deck, but did little damage to the upper decks. However, below the waterline, and out of sight of the crew on the bridge, the iceberg punched a series of gashes and holes along 250 ft (76 m) of the hull.

FIRST OFFICER MURDOCH
William Murdoch was in charge of the bridge at the time of the impact. He ordered the change of direction and closed the watertight doors. Later Murdoch was told to call all the passengers up on deck ready for evacuation into the lifeboats.

AT THE WHEEL
Quartermaster Robert Hichens was at the wheel when the collision occurred. First Officer Murdoch ordered him to turn the wheel hard to starboard (right), swinging the bow to the port (left) of the iceberg. That was all Hichens had time to do.

Wheel was linked to the steering mechanism in the stern above the rudder

To the lifeboats

At 12:05 a.m., 25 minutes after the collision, Captain Smith realized the extent of the damage to the *Titanic* and gave the order to uncover the lifeboats and prepare to abandon ship. For the next two hours, total confusion reigned; there had been no lifeboat drill since leaving Southampton, and neither passengers nor crew knew where to go or what to do in the circumstances. Many felt it was safer to remain on deck than to be lowered into the freezing Atlantic aboard a lifeboat. Tragically, not one officer realized that the lifeboats could be lowered fully laden. Had they done so, a total of 1,178 people could have been saved, rather than 706.

WOMEN AND CHILDREN FIRST?
The rule on board the *Titanic*—and on all other ships at that time—was to save women and children first. But some men did escape, many more from the starboard- (right-) side lifeboats than from the port- (left-) side ones. In many lifeboats, "first come, first saved" was the rule.

"As I was put into the boat, he (Mr. Daniel Marvin) cried to me, 'It's all right, little girl. You go. I will stay.' As our boat shoved off he threw me a kiss, and that was the last I saw of him."

TITANIC HONEYMOONER MRS. DANIEL MARVIN

THOMAS ANDREWS
Within minutes of the *Titanic* striking the iceberg, Thomas Andrews—managing director of Harland Wolff and builder of the ship—toured below the decks with Captain Smith. Andrews calculated that the ship had two hours, at most, before it sank. Later, however, he failed to point out that the new davits (lowering devices) were strong enough to launch the lifeboats fully laden.

BUOYANCY AID
Life jackets were stowed in every cabin aboard the *Titanic*, and there was one for each passenger and crew member. Some people, however, chose not to wear one or did not manage to find one in time. The life jackets were buoyant enough to keep a fully clothed person afloat, but they were very bulky to wear and offered little protection against the extreme cold.

Cork floats covered with thick canvas

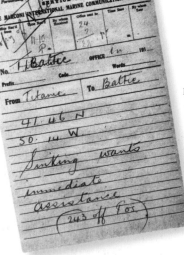

IN DISTRESS
As the lifeboats filled up, the two radio operators—Jack Phillips and Harold Bride—tirelessly sent out distress messages stating that the *Titanic* was sinking and asking for help. Among those ships that picked up the *Titanic*'s pleas for assistance were the *Olympic*, the *Baltic*, and the *Carpathia*.

One by one

One by one the lifeboats were lowered from the *Titanic*, starting with number 7 (see below) at 12:45 a.m., and finishing with collapsible D at 2:05 a.m.; the last two collapsibles floated away from the ship as it sank. The total capacity of all 20 boats was 1,178; the figures below show that about 862 people managed to get into a lifeboat. However, according to the US Senate report, the total number of people saved was only 706, which suggests that some people exaggerated the numbers in each boat to avoid accusations that they deliberately left people to drown.

THE COLLAPSIBLES
Two collapsible lifeboats were stored, flat and upturned, on deck, and the other two were stowed on the roof of the officers' quarters. The collapsibles had flat, double-bottomed floors and low canvas-topped sides, which could be pulled up to a height of 3 ft (1 m) and fixed into position.

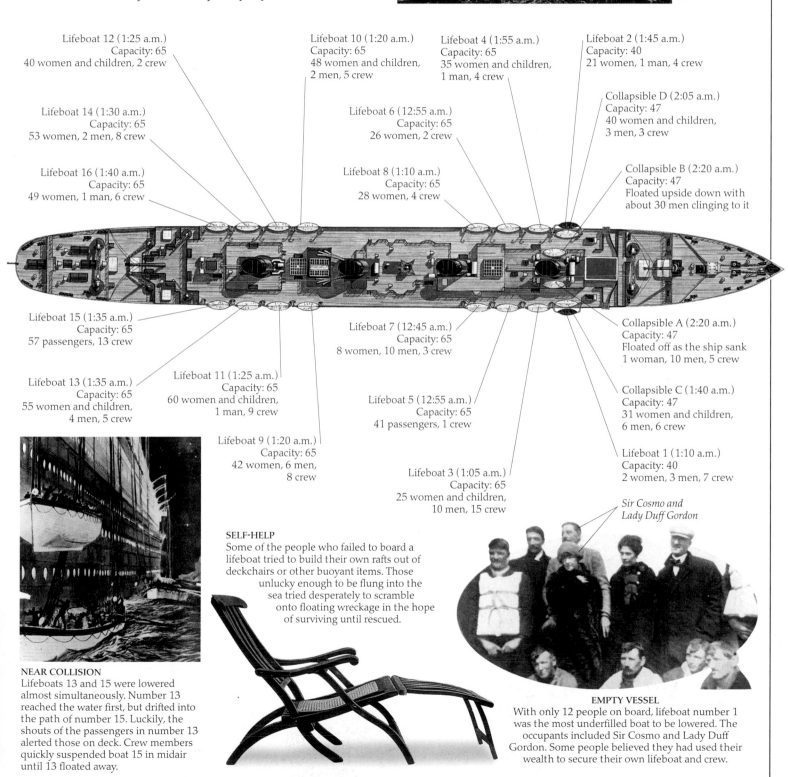

Lifeboat 12 (1:25 a.m.)
Capacity: 65
40 women and children, 2 crew

Lifeboat 14 (1:30 a.m.)
Capacity: 65
53 women, 2 men, 8 crew

Lifeboat 16 (1:40 a.m.)
Capacity: 65
49 women, 1 man, 6 crew

Lifeboat 15 (1:35 a.m.)
Capacity: 65
57 passengers, 13 crew

Lifeboat 13 (1:35 a.m.)
Capacity: 65
55 women and children, 4 men, 5 crew

Lifeboat 11 (1:25 a.m.)
Capacity: 65
60 women and children, 1 man, 9 crew

Lifeboat 9 (1:20 a.m.)
Capacity: 65
42 women, 6 men, 8 crew

Lifeboat 10 (1:20 a.m.)
Capacity: 65
48 women and children, 2 men, 5 crew

Lifeboat 6 (12:55 a.m.)
Capacity: 65
26 women, 2 crew

Lifeboat 8 (1:10 a.m.)
Capacity: 65
28 women, 4 crew

Lifeboat 7 (12:45 a.m.)
Capacity: 65
8 women, 10 men, 3 crew

Lifeboat 5 (12:55 a.m.)
Capacity: 65
41 passengers, 1 crew

Lifeboat 3 (1:05 a.m.)
Capacity: 65
25 women and children, 10 men, 15 crew

Lifeboat 4 (1:55 a.m.)
Capacity: 65
35 women and children, 1 man, 4 crew

Lifeboat 2 (1:45 a.m.)
Capacity: 40
21 women, 1 man, 4 crew

Collapsible D (2:05 a.m.)
Capacity: 47
40 women and children, 3 men, 3 crew

Collapsible B (2:20 a.m.)
Capacity: 47
Floated upside down with about 30 men clinging to it

Collapsible A (2:20 a.m.)
Capacity: 47
Floated off as the ship sank
1 woman, 10 men, 5 crew

Collapsible C (1:40 a.m.)
Capacity: 47
31 women and children, 6 men, 6 crew

Lifeboat 1 (1:10 a.m.)
Capacity: 40
2 women, 3 men, 7 crew

Sir Cosmo and Lady Duff Gordon

NEAR COLLISION
Lifeboats 13 and 15 were lowered almost simultaneously. Number 13 reached the water first, but drifted into the path of number 15. Luckily, the shouts of the passengers in number 13 alerted those on deck. Crew members quickly suspended boat 15 in midair until 13 floated away.

SELF-HELP
Some of the people who failed to board a lifeboat tried to build their own rafts out of deckchairs or other buoyant items. Those unlucky enough to be flung into the sea tried desperately to scramble onto floating wreckage in the hope of surviving until rescued.

EMPTY VESSEL
With only 12 people on board, lifeboat number 1 was the most underfilled boat to be lowered. The occupants included Sir Cosmo and Lady Duff Gordon. Some people believed they had used their wealth to secure their own lifeboat and crew.

Slowly sinking

As THE LIFEBOATS SLID down the side of the ship, a flurry of activity took place on deck. The radio operators sent out distress signals. Officers on the bridge flashed messages by Morse signal lamp and fired rockets high into the night sky to attract the attention of any passing ships. Yet, despite all these actions, it was hard for many people to believe that this vast liner was capable of sinking. Some, such as Benjamin Guggenheim (below), reconciled themselves to their fate, but most believed that help would arrive long before the ship sank.

Signaling lamp

SIGNALING
Shortly before the first rocket signal was fired, both Captain Smith and Fourth Officer Boxhall spotted the lights of a nearby ship. Boxhall attempted to attract the ship's attention by flashing the CQD ("come quick, danger") distress signal. But the passing ship did not respond and its lights soon faded from view. For many years the ship was believed to have been the *Californian*, but more recent evidence suggests that it may have been a ship illegally hunting seals.

A GENTLEMAN
Once the last lifeboat had departed, millionaire Benjamin Guggenheim realized that he was not going to be saved and returned to his cabin. There, he and his valet (personal attendant) dressed in evening suits and returned to the top deck. "We've dressed in our best and are prepared to go down like gentlemen," Guggenheim was heard to say before he was lost with the *Titanic*.

Rocket signals explode in the sky

LIGHTING UP THE SKY
In order to attract any nearby ships, Fourth Officer Boxhall fired the first of about eight powerful rocket signals at 12:45 a.m. Each signal—sent up at five-minute intervals—was launched from the bridge and soared 800 ft (240 m) into the air before exploding into a shower of light. There was no set procedure for the firing of distress signals, but it was internationally agreed that the regularity of the rockets would distinguish them from a firework display.

A panic-stricken passenger slides down a rope into an already overcrowded lifeboat in the film A Night To Remember *(1958)*

DESPERATE MEASURES
As the final lifeboats were lowered, a number of people tried to jump ship by sliding down the ropes or leaping from the lower decks. Others jumped into the water, hoping to scramble aboard later. A few lucky people managed to stow away in a lifeboat on deck and were only detected once afloat.

JACK PHILLIPS
The first distress signals that wireless operator Jack Phillips sent out were the CQD signals. After a while, his assistant suggested he try using the new SOS signal. At 12:45 a.m. Phillips sent the first SOS signal ever to be transmitted from a ship in danger.

Final radio message sent by the Titanic

CQD = SOS
The first radio distress signal was CQD. In 1906, the International Radio Telegraphic Convention in Berlin, Germany, created the SOS signal, chosen because the three letters were simple to transmit by Morse code. In 1908, SOS became the official distress signal, but, until the *Titanic* disaster, most Marconi operators continued to use the old signal.

Key is pressed to tap out messages in Morse code

Morse code SOS

Morse code CQD

COMMUNICATING IN CODE
Morse code was invented in 1838 by Samuel Morse and was one of the best methods of signaling at sea until the arrival of the radiotelephone. Each letter of a word is represented as a series of short or long radio signals or flashes of light.

Lights still illuminate the Titanic *to draw the attention of any passing ships*

"It's the new call, and it might be your last chance to send it."

JUNIOR WIRELESS OPERATOR, HAROLD BRIDE, TO JACK PHILLIPS

Stern rises high out of the water

The final moments

As **THE** *TITANIC* **SLIPPED** lower and lower into the water, those left on board when the last of the lifeboats had departed were either gripped by a sense of panic or resigned to their fate. Some tried to make rafts out of deck chairs and other items of furniture, while others prayed for rescue and comforted their loved ones. The noise on board soon became deafening as the contents of the ship broke free of their fixtures and crashed forward. As the ship plunged deeper into the sea, the stern rose up in the air, causing a tidal wave of passengers to fall off the deck, some into the wreckage, others into the icy sea. Out on the ocean, those lucky survivors in the lifeboats averted their eyes as the *Titanic* met its horrific end.

Kate Winslet and Leonardo DiCaprio run for their lives in the 1997 film *Titanic*

AGAINST THE TIDE
At about 2:15 a.m., water crashed through the glass dome and poured down the grand staircase, sweeping aside those fleeing to the top deck in search of safety.

Titanic's stern rose up vertically for about 30 seconds before disappearing beneath the sea

Funnels and other equipment on deck broke free and crashed beneath the waves

IN TIME OF NEED
One of the second-class passengers was Father Thomas Byles, a Roman Catholic priest. As the ship sank, he heard confessions and led prayers at the stern end of the boat deck. Like many of his flock, he lost his life.

LAST MOMENTS
At 2:18 a.m. the *Titanic's* lights finally went out as the boilers were completely submerged. The ship was almost vertical, its bow diving down toward the seabed, its stern rising up into the night sky. At this point, the ship snapped between the back two funnels, causing the stern section to break free and right itself briefly before it too began to sink. At 2:20 a.m. the *Titanic* finally slipped from view.

Officer Lightoller fires warning shots into the panicking crowd in the film A Night To Remember

PANIC STATIONS

In case of serious disturbances on board, pistols were kept in a safe for use by senior officers. During the launching of the lifeboats, gunshots were fired into the air to prevent panicking crowds from swamping the boats. Intriguingly, there are also reports that an officer actually shot two men dead, and then turned the gun on himself, although the evidence for this remains unverified.

ALL ALONE

Adrift among the icebergs, the passengers on board the lifeboats must have felt very vulnerable and alone. With no lights visible from passing ships, many survivors took turns at rowing to keep their spirits up and to keep their blood circulating.

Propeller and rudder high up in the air

"Not until the last five minutes did the awful realization come that the end was at hand. The lights became dim and went out, but we could see. Slowly, ever so slowly, the surface of the water seemed to come up toward us."

ROBERT DANIEL, PASSENGER

BLASTED TO SAFETY

First-class passenger Colonel Archibald Gracie was swept off the deck as the ship plummeted beneath the sea. At first he was dragged under by the suction of the sinking ship; but then, suddenly, he was blown clear by a gust of air escaping from a ventilation shaft and managed to clamber on board the upturned collapsible lifeboat B.

Lifeboats rowed clear of the sinking ship to keep from being dragged down by the ship's suction

Heroes and heroines

THE EXTREME AND DANGEROUS circumstances that all the passengers and crew faced brought forward some remarkable acts of heroism and self-sacrifice. Women such as Molly Brown and the Countess of Rothes were used to having everything done for them. But they forgot any idea of social rank and worked the oars on the lifeboats, proving themselves to be more than a match for any of the men on board. Others, such as Isidor and Ida Straus, both in their sixties, chose to stay together on the ship. Down in the boiler rooms, the firemen and stokers worked until the end to keep the lights burning to attract any passing ships. Up on deck, the two wireless operators sent out emergency signals for as long as possible. And all the time the band played on.

COUNTESS OF ROTHES
In lifeboat number 8, the Countess of Rothes took her turn at the oars before handling the tiller for most of the night. In gratitude for her hard work that night, the crew member in charge of the boat, Thomas Jones, later presented her with the lifeboat number plate mounted on a plaque.

THE UNSINKABLE MOLLY BROWN
US millionairess Molly Brown was one of 26 women on board lifeboat number 6. In charge was Quartermaster Hichens, who refused to order the women to row; so Molly Brown took command. She threatened to throw Hichens overboard and rowed furiously toward the rescue ship. Mrs. Brown's heroic determination earned her the title of "the unsinkable Molly Brown."

"When I saw the way she was carrying herself and heard the quiet determined way she spoke to the others, I knew she was more of a man than any we had on board."

THOMAS JONES OF LIFEBOAT 8 PRAISES THE COUNTESS OF ROTHES

Names of 38 engineers lost with the Titanic

IN MEMORIAM
The town most affected by the disaster was Southampton, England, where most of the crew lived. On April 22, 1914, a monument to the ship's engineers (right) was unveiled in the city's East Park. More than 100,000 people attended the unveiling. A year later, a smaller memorial to the steward was unveiled on Southampton Common; this memorial was later moved to a local church.

AND THE BAND PLAYED ON

The *Titanic* had two bands—a string quintet, led by violinist Wally Hartley, that played for first-class passengers, and a string and piano trio that played outside the à la carte restaurant. After the collision, the musicians assembled in the first-class lounge and played a selection of ragtimes and other songs to keep passengers' spirits up. They played on until the very end, going down with their ship. There is still debate over the final piece the band played—either the hymn *Nearer, My God, To Thee* or the slow waltz *Songe d'Automne*.

Captain Smith is shown here swimming toward crowded collapsible lifeboat B

Extract from the hymn Nearer, My God, To Thee, *believed to be the final piece of music played aboard the* Titanic

CAPTAIN SMITH

The last minutes of Captain Smith's life are largely uncertain because he went down with his ship. Several survivors claimed that he swam close to the upturned collapsible lifeboat B but turned away when he realized how overcrowded its hull was. Others alleged that he handed over a baby that he had rescued from the sea, although there is no proof that this story is true.

TOGETHER FOREVER

Wealthy passenger Isidor Straus was the founder of the world-famous Macy's department store in New York. Because of his age, he was offered the chance to board a lifeboat, but turned it down. His wife, Ida, refused to leave the ship without him, saying, "I will not be separated from my husband. As we have lived, so we will die together." Both went down with the ship.

Engineer at work

41

Racing to the rescue

At 12:25 A.M. THE WIRELESS OPERATOR on board the 15,192-ton (13,782-metric ton) RMS *Carpathia* picked up a distress message from the *Titanic*. The ship, en route from New York to the Mediterranean, turned around immediately and traveled, as fast as possible, 58 miles (93 km) northwest to the distressed liner. Captain Rostron prepared his ship to receive survivors, although he had no idea how many to expect. Doctors on board the *Carpathia* were put on standby, steward and cooks prepared accommodation and food, and rockets were fired every 15 minutes to signal the ship's approach. Rostron's immediate concern, however, was ice, for the same iceberg that had sunk the *Titanic* could easily sink his ship, too.

ROWING TO SAFETY
The icefield surrounding the survivors meant that it was too dangerous for the *Carpathia* to move in close to the lifeboats. The exhausted survivors, therefore, had to row toward the stationary ship. It took the *Carpathia* four hours to rescue all of the survivors because the lifeboats were scattered over a 4-mile (6.4-km) area.

RUTH BECKER
Second-class passenger Ruth Becker was only 12 years old when she found herself separated from her mother and her younger brother and sister. But she displayed remarkable bravery when aboard lifeboat 13 by helping to distribute blankets and by talking, through an interpreter, to a distraught German mother who had been separated from her child. Both the Beckers and the German family were reunited on board the *Carpathia*.

Masthead lights told survivors that help was on its way

Smoke spewed from Carpathia's funnel as the ship raced to rescue Titanic's survivors

IN SIGHT
At 4:00 a.m., the *Carpathia* reached the *Titanic*'s last reported position and cut its engines. In the gloom, a green light flickered from lifeboat number 2, where Fourth Officer Boxhall was in charge. Once on board the *Carpathia*, he confirmed the worst to Captain Rostron, who then faced the grim task of organizing the rescue operation.

LOOKING FOR SURVIVORS
Only one of the lifeboats—number 14, commanded by Fifth Officer Lowe (above)—went back to look for survivors. His boat pulled four people from the sea. All the other boats rowed away from the scene because most of the occupants feared being sucked down by the sinking ship or swamped by those fighting for their lives in the sea. Only 12 people in total were picked up, despite most lifeboats having room for many more.

Survivors burned paper and waved their hands to attract attention

Lifeboats hidden among the floating ice

ELECTRIC SPARK
At the time of the *Titanic* tragedy, 42-year-old Captain Arthur Rostron of the *Carpathia* was very experienced, having been at sea since the age of 13. He was renowned for his quick decision-making and energetic leadership. Out of respect for his abilities, his Cunard shipmates nicknamed him the "electric spark."

Survivors await their turn to board the Carpathia

SAFE AT LAST
The first survivor, Elizabeth Allen, clambered up a rope ladder to board the *Carpathia* at 4:10 a.m., just under two hours after the *Titanic* sank. Some survivors were well enough to climb rope ladders, others had to be winched to safety in a boatswain's chair (wooden seat suspended from two ropes). A few young children were scooped up in mail sacks.

Gangway door open to receive survivors

"After we were picked up on the Carpathia *my mother came to me, 'cos every time a lifeboat came I went to see if my father was on it… he wasn't, so my mother turned round and said, 'You've lost your father, you won't see your father anymore… he's gone.'"*

EDITH HAISMAN

THANK YOU
Survivors of the disaster joined together to buy a silver cup for Captain Rostron and 320 medals for his crew. The reverse side of each medal bore the crew member's name and the inscription: "Presented to the captain, officers, and crew of RMS *Carpathia*, in recognition of gallant and heroic services, from the survivors of the SS *Titanic*, April 15th 1912".

Blankets to keep the survivors warm

ALL HANDS ON DECK
As the survivors clambered on board the *Carpathia*, they were met by passengers and crew offering blankets, a nip of brandy, and hot food and drinks. Some survivors were taken to cabins, others huddled on the deck and tried to come to terms with the ordeal they had just endured. Everyone noticed how silent the ship was despite all the activity on board.

Medal shows the Carpathia *sailing through ice*

Awaiting news

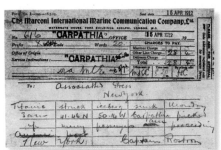

THE WORST CONFIRMED
Captain Rostron waited until all survivors were safely on board the *Carpathia* before broadcasting any messages. Wireless contact was initially restricted to sending a list of survivors and their messages: requests from the press for information were ignored. Finally, at 8:20 p.m. on Monday evening, the captain sent a brief telegram confirming the worst to Associated Press in New York.

A YOUNG RADIO ENTHUSIAST in New York picked up the *Titanic*'s faint distress signals in the early hours of Monday April 15. The signals were also detected in Newfoundland, Canada. The word was out that the *Titanic* was in trouble, but other messages during the day appeared to contradict this fact. It was not until 6:16 p.m. New York time that the *Olympic*, the *Titanic*'s sister ship, confirmed that the *Titanic* had sunk. Two hours later, the rescue ship, *Carpathia*, broke its radio silence and announced it was bringing survivors into New York.

WAITING FOR NEWS
As news filtered through on Monday, crowds of concerned relatives and bystanders formed outside the White Star offices in New York, London (right), and Southampton. Detailed information was hard to come by, and it took some days before the first, incomplete list of survivors was posted up in New York.

For Hascoe, read C. H. Pascoe

For Ross, read H. Ross, cook

MISTAKEN IDENTITIES
On Wednesday, a list of saved crew members was posted up outside the White Star offices in Southampton, where 699 of the 898 crew lived. In the confusion, names were spelled incorrectly and initials left off, raising some relatives' hopes unnecessarily. Sheets of corrected names slowly appeared, finally confirming who had survived and who had been lost.

READ ALL ABOUT IT
The cries of newspaper boys shouting out the headlines brought home to many people the scale of the disaster. In the absence of firm news from the White Star Line or from the rescue ship, *Carpathia*, worried relatives read the newspapers closely, searching for any scrap of information that might tell them about their loved ones.

TITANIC DISASTER GREAT LOSS OF LIFE EVENING NEWS

"I have read the papers trying to get some hope, but all fail now. I shall pray for the body. He was so good to me."

TITANIC SURVIVOR WRITES ABOUT HER HUSBAND

Monday's New York Evening Sun reported that all passengers were safe

Tuesday morning's Chicago Daily Tribune confirms the full extent of the horror, although many details are still missing

Although news of the disaster spread rapidly around the world, it did not always make front page news

AROUND THE WORLD

The *Titanic* disaster dominated the world's newspapers for days, although many of the early stories were vague and often contradictory. Most papers erred on the side of caution, not believing that such a disaster could have occurred. They even printed as fact rumors that the *Titanic* was being towed to Halifax, Nova Scotia, and that all its passengers were safe.

GOOD NEWS, BAD NEWS

Many women in Southampton lost a number of male relatives in the disaster. Mrs. Rosina Hurst (seen on the left) lost her father-in-law, although her husband, fireman Walter Hurst, survived. Sharing the news with her is her aunt, also in mourning clothes.

Lost and found

Mrs. Goldsmith, pictured shortly after the disaster, wearing two wedding rings

How MANY PEOPLE lost their lives in the *Titanic* disaster will never be known for sure, since the total number of passengers and crew on board has never been officially established. The US Senate investigation put the total losses at 1,517 (shown in the table below), while the British enquiry calculated 1,490. Some authorities put the losses as high as 1,635. But whatever the figures, the human tragedy of lives lost and families torn apart makes each survivor's story all the more poignant. Whether rich or poor, famous or unknown, every one of the 705 survivors had a remarkable tale to tell.

RING TWICE
As Mrs. Goldsmith stepped into the lifeboat with her son, Frankie, family friend Thomas Theobald slipped off his wedding ring and asked her to pass it on to his wife. Mr. Theobald died; Mrs. Goldsmith was photographed by the *Detroit News* on April 26 still wearing the two rings.

Honeymooners Mr. and Mrs. Harder

HORRIFIC HONEYMOONS
Eight newlywed couples chose to take their honeymoon on the *Titanic*'s maiden voyage, although only two couples lived to tell the tale. Here Mr. and Mrs. George Harder rest on *Carpathia*'s boat deck, sharing the horrors of the night before with Mrs. Hays, a fellow survivor.

Survivor Mrs. Clara Hays, who lost her husband, Charles Hays, president of Canada's Grand Trunk Railroad

BABY MILLVINA
Aged only seven weeks at the time of the disaster, Millvina Dean was the youngest survivor of the *Titanic* disaster. Her mother, Ettie, and brother, Bert, also survived; her father perished. In later life, Millvina opened the exhibition of *Titanic* artefacts held in Greenwich, England, in 1994.

FIRST CLASS
One-hundred-and-forty-five women and children survived, ten women and one child died. Of the men, 54 survived and 119 died. In total, 60 percent of first-class passengers survived.

199
130

SECOND CLASS
One-hundred-and-four women and children survived, 24 died. Of the men, only 15 survived and 142 died. In total, 42 percent of second-class passengers survived.

119
166

UNDER COVER
Second-class passenger Louis Hoffmann gave the impression he was taking his recently orphaned children to start a new life in the United States. In reality, "Louis Hoffmann" was Michel Navratil, who had separated from his wife and abducted his sons. The boys survived the disaster and were eventually reunited with their mother.

Michel, aged 3

THIRD CLASS
One-hundred-and-five women and children survived, 119 died. Of the men, only 69 survived and 417 died. In total, 25 percent of third-class passengers survived.

174
536

Edmond, aged 2

Table showing how the numbers of people lost and saved varied greatly among the three classes and crew.

Saved
Lost

CREW
Twenty women survived, three died. Of the men, 193 survived and 682 died. In total, 24 percent of the crew survived.

213
685

LIMPING HOME

On arrival in New York, Harold Bride's feet were so frostbitten that he had to be carried ashore. One of the heroes of the disaster, Bride had kept sending distress signals until minutes before the *Titanic* sank. He then resumed duties on board the *Carpathia*.

Harold Bride's ankles were badly injured during the escape, and his feet were frostbitten by the icy sea

REST IN PEACE

On Saturday, April 20, less than one week after the disaster, Canon Kenneth Hind conducted a funeral service on board the *Mackay-Bennett*. Twenty-four people, too disfigured to be identified, were sewn into weighted sacks and given a dignified burial at sea. Further services were held over the next month as more victims were found.

Hat removed out of respect for the dead

WRITING HOME

Many survivors wrote long and detailed letters to friends or family recounting their ordeal. Mary Hewlett, a second-class passenger who was in lifeboat number 13, wrote, "I had some long letters I had written to my girls… and I gave them to be burned, sheet by sheet, as signals. The dawn came at about 4:30 a.m. and then we saw dozens of icebergs and the new Moon in a pink haze—it was a most wonderful sight and soon after that, at about 5 o'clock, we saw the mast lights of the *Carpathia* on the horizon."

AT GOD'S SERVICE

The Reverend John Harper was on his way from London to hold a series of Baptist revival meetings at the Moody Church in Chicago, where he had preached the previous winter. Harper's two traveling companions—his young daughter, Nina, and a relative, Jessie Leitch—both survived, but he went down with the ship.

Body is pulled from the sea into Mackay-Bennett's rowboat

GATHERING THE DEAD

The gruesome task of collecting bodies from the sea was conducted by ships from Halifax, Nova Scotia. The *Mackay-Bennett* carried tons of ice to preserve the bodies, more than 100 coffins, and 40 embalmers. Over the course of six weeks, 328 bodies were found; 119 of these were buried at sea and the rest returned to Halifax, either for burial or to be claimed by relatives.

Lessons learned

Life buoy

FOUR DAYS AFTER THE *TITANIC* SANK, the first official inquiry into the disaster, chaired by Senator William Alden Smith, opened in New York and lasted for 17 days. The 82 witnesses called to the stand included: White Star chairman, Bruce Ismay; Guglielmo Marconi; lookout Frederick Fleet; and Captain Lord of the *Californian*. Two weeks later, the British inquiry began under Lord Mersey, a former High Court judge. Although both inquiries covered much the same ground, their main difference was motive: the US inquiry was conducted by politicians looking for someone to blame, while the British inquiry was conducted by lawyers and technical experts trying to establish the facts to ensure there was no repetition of the disaster. Both inquiries made much the same recommendations, calling for ships to be safer and built to higher standards, to make effective use of radio, and to carry sufficient lifeboats for everyone on board.

Titanic *survivors line up to receive shipwreck pay*

THE FORGOTTEN CREW

Under the White Star Line's conditions of service, the *Titanic*'s crew ceased to be paid at 2:20 a.m. on April 15, the moment the ship sank. Those who appeared before the US inquiry received some expenses, but most were shipped directly home by White Star with little or no financial aid. Many of the surviving crew had to rely on charity or emergency shipwreck payments from the Sailors' and Firemen's Union until they could find another job.

WHO WAS TO BLAME?

The US inquiry had no doubt that Captain Smith was to blame for the tragedy because of his "indifference to danger" and his "overconfidence and neglect." The hearing also blamed Captain Lord of the *Californian*, for failing to come to the rescue, and the British Board of Trade for not updating its lifeboat regulations and for its poor inspection standards during the ship's construction. In comparison, the British inquiry agreed that the *Titanic* was traveling too fast but did not find Captain Smith negligent, nor did it criticize the Board of Trade.

The British *Titanic* inquiry in progress

Scale model of the Titanic

Witness Sir Cosmo Duff Gordon gives evidence in the stand

Presiding judge, Lord Mersey

ICE PATROL

One of the lasting results of the collision was the agreement, in 1914, by 16 North Atlantic nations to establish the International Ice Patrol to look out for icebergs in the North Atlantic shipping lanes. Today, the patrol uses ships and airplanes equipped with radar, underwater sonar equipment, and the latest forecasting technology to log all icebergs and report their existence to every ship in the area. Many lives have been saved as a result of this patrol.

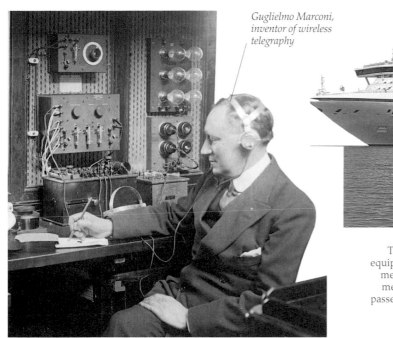

Guglielmo Marconi, inventor of wireless telegraphy

Lifeboats hang beneath the promenade decks of this modern liner, allowing passengers a clear view across the sea

MORE LIFEBOATS

The main recommendation of both inquiries was that every ship be equipped with enough lifeboats to accommodate every passenger and crew member, and that regular lifeboat drills be held. For existing ships, this meant placing more lifeboats on deck, reducing the space available for passengers to walk on the upper decks and restricting their view of the sea. Modern ships are designed to overcome these problems.

ON AIR

Both inquiries recommended that every ship be equipped with a radio and that radio contact be maintained 24 hours a day. The inquiries also advised that ship radios should adhere to international regulations. Previously a novelty enjoyed by wealthy passengers only, radio contact now became a major navigational and safety aid at sea.

LAST OF THE LINE

Although the *Titanic* proved that watertight bulkheads could not prevent a ship from sinking, the designers of the Italian luxury transatlantic liner *Andrea Doria* claimed their ship was unsinkable. But after a collision with the *Stockholm*, in 1956, the ship sank when only one of its 11 compartments flooded. The reason was that the ship was light on fuel and ballast (heavy material used to stabilize ships) and was floating high in the water. As the bulkhead filled with water, the ship keeled to one side, and water poured in above the watertight compartments.

It took several hours for the Andrea Doria *to plunge 240 ft (73 m) beneath the sea*

End of an era

WHEN THE *TITANIC* WAS BUILT, it was to be the second in a trio of luxury liners intended to dominate the world of transatlantic travel. Only one of the three—the *Olympic*—lived up to White Star Line's dream. The *Titanic* sank on its maiden voyage. The *Britannic* was only ever used for military service, and its entire working life was less than one year. The *Olympic* was the exception. After the *Titanic* tragedy, the *Olympic* was equipped with extra safety precautions and cruised the North Atlantic for more than 20 years as both a civilian and a military ship. In 1934, the White Star Line merged with its old rival, Cunard, and within a year the *Olympic* sailed its final voyage. The dream was over.

NOT SO GIGANTIC
The third of the great White Star Liners was originally to be called *Gigantic*, but it was renamed *Britannic* to avoid comparisons with the *Titanic*. With the recent tragedy in mind, the *Britannic* was equipped with a double-skinned hull, bulkheads up to B deck, and giant davits (lowering devices) capable of launching enough lifeboats for everyone on board.

TROOP SHIP
In the first few months of World War I, the *Olympic* continued to take passengers across the Atlantic and even rescued the crew of a British battleship that had struck a mine off the coast of Ireland. In September 1915, the *Olympic* was commissioned as a naval transport ship and, over a three-year period, ferried 119,000 troops and civilians. The survivor of three submarine attacks, the ship earned itself the nickname "Old Reliable."

WHITE STAR LINE

R.M.S. "OLYMPIC" 46,359 Tons.
(The largest British Steamer)

"Dazzle" paint camouflage to confuse enemy submarines

Deck lined with sufficient lifeboats to carry all passengers and crew members

Friends and relatives wave to passengers aboard the Olympic *as it departs from New York*

THE BOOM YEARS
After a postwar refit, the *Olympic* returned to civilian service in July 1920. For the next 15 years the ship made hundreds of voyages across the Atlantic and carried many thousands of passengers. The ship had only one major accident when, on May 15, 1934, it struck a lightship in heavy fog. Seven of the lightship's 11 crew members were killed. By 1935, the *Olympic* had become dated and, in March of that year, made its final voyage before it was sold, stripped of its fixtures, and scrapped.

IN SERVICE
World War I broke out only six months after the *Britannic*'s launch on February 26, 1914. The ship was hurriedly transformed into a fully equipped hospital ship with dormitories and operating rooms on each deck and entered war service in December 1915.

Red crosses painted on the side of the hull indicate that the Britannic *is a hospital ship*

Volunteer nurse's uniform

Massive hole ripped out of the Britannic's *port side*

NURSE JESSOP
Most of those who lost their lives on the *Britannic* were actually afloat in lifeboats, but were killed by the rotating propellers when an attempt was made to restart the engines. One of the lucky survivors was Nurse Violet Jessop (above), who had already escaped death as a stewardess aboard the *Titanic*.

TO THE SEABED
On November 21, 1916, the *Britannic* was steaming northward through the Kea Channel, southeast of Athens, on her way to pick up wounded Allied soldiers on the Isle of Lemnos. A sudden explosion ripped the ship open and sank it within an hour. No one knows what caused the explosion, but it is likely that the ship struck a mine.

French walnut paneling from the first-class à la carte restaurant of the RMS Olympic

AFTERLIFE
Many of the carved wooden panels and other fixtures from the *Olympic* were removed from the ship before it was scrapped and stored in a barn in northern England. Rediscovered 56 years later, the fixtures were offered for sale and now furnish the interiors of hotels, factories, and private homes across England.

Search and discovery

FOR SCIENTISTS ON BOARD *KNORR*, the ship searching for the wreck of the *Titanic*, the night of August 31, 1985, promised to be as uneventful as any other. For two futile months, the uncrewed submersible *Argo* had scoured the murky depths of the North Atlantic Ocean. Then, just after midnight on September 1, small pieces of metal began to show up on the ship's monitors. At first the team saw only the wreckage of a boiler, but it was instantly recognizable as one of the *Titanic*'s. The camera followed a trail of objects until, suddenly, the huge black shadow of the ship's hull came into view. Seventy-three years after its tragic loss, the *Titanic* had been found.

The shallow Grand Banks of Newfoundland lie just to the north of the wreck

Seabed of thick mud strewn with boulders and small rocks

RESTING PLACE
The *Titanic* was located at 41°43'N, 49°56'W, 480 miles (770 km) southeast of Newfoundland, Canada. The wreck lies on the gently sloping seabed overlooking a small canyon, which scientists named the Titanic Canyon in 1980.

1,600 ft (500m)

3,300 ft 1,000 (m)

Model of the bow section of the *Titanic* wreck

Bow and stern sections cut almost clean apart

6,500 ft (2,000 m)

THE WRECK
The bow and stern sections of the ship lie 1,970 ft (600 m) apart on the seabed, facing in opposite directions. Both are upright, the bow section having plowed 65 ft (20 m) into the mud. Despite the impact, the bow section is remarkably intact.

9,800 ft (3,000 m)

HOSTILE WATERS
The *Titanic* lies in 12,470 ft (3,800 m) of water. At this depth, there is no light and the temperature is no more than 36°F (2°C). No plants grow at this depth, and few fish can survive the intense pressure and cold.

GIGANTIC BOILERS
As the ship sank, most of the 29 vast boilers broke away and crashed around inside the hull. Only five, however, broke completely free of the ship and were later found in the field of debris. The remaining 24 boilers are probably still within the bow section.

RUSTY BOW
Over the years, layers and layers of rust have covered a fitting on the bow of the *Titanic*, making it appear like a figurehead. In reality, the fitting was to secure the forestay (support) that held up the foremast.

13,000 ft (4,000 m)

PICKING UP THE PIECES
In July 1987, a team of French scientists sailed to the site of the *Titanic* to carry out more thorough investigations. The expedition worked from the surface ship *Nadir* (above), and a crew of three explored the seabed in the submersible *Nautile* (right). Using the submersible's mechanical arms, the crew scooped 1,800 objects from the seabed.

Powerful spotlights illuminate the wreck

Robotic arm for picking up objects

Crew sit inside a titanium sphere

UNDERWATER EXPLORER
Nautile, the submersible used in the 1987 *Titanic* expedition, measured only 27 ft (8 m) in length. Its three-person crew—pilot, co-pilot, and observer – took 90 minutes to reach the seabed and could stay down for up to eight hours before they had to return to the surface.

ALL ABOARD
Life on board *Nautile* was cramped and hot. The three-person crew lay on their sides, looking out on the wreck through the small portholes. Lights illuminated the scene outside; video cameras recorded it for posterity.

Portholes are filled with extra-thick, curved Plexiglas®, which becomes flat during the dive due to the water pressure

Foremast lies collapsed over the deck

Anchor crane still stands upright at the bow; behind it are the two massive anchor chains

Titanic's starboard anchor can still be seen in its original position

TOPPLED TELEGRAPH
This telegraph was among the many items photographed by *Argo*. Originally mounted on the docking bridge at the stern of the ship, the telegraph was used to communicate with the engine room when maneuvering the ship in and out of port.

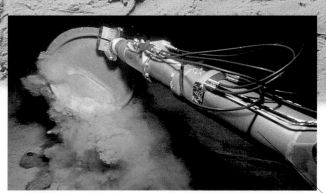

PEEPING INTO THE PAST
Among the many items picked up from the wreck by the 1987 expedition was one of the ship's many portholes. Porcelain plates, cutlery, light fixtures, an empty safe, a statue of a cherub from the grand staircase—even a chamber pot—were all scooped up from the seafloor.

Nautile's arms have several attachments—a sucker, a gripper, and a shovel—for gathering objects from the seabed

Pieces of the puzzle

THE DISCOVERY OF THE *TITANIC* wreck and the salvage of artifacts from the seabed have solved some, but not all, of the unanswered questions that surround the fatal voyage. We now know that the hull broke up as it sank, and that the steel used in its construction was not strong enough to withstand the cold waters of the North Atlantic. We also know that the ship sank some 13 miles (21 km) away from the position estimated at the time of the disaster. This casts doubt on various accounts of which ships were in the area and able to come to the rescue. The story of the *Titanic* still excites controversy, almost 100 years after the event. Many people think that recovering items from the wreck site is like robbing a grave, and that the *Titanic* should be left in peace. Others want to raise as much of the ship and its contents as possible in order to put them on display. Whatever the final outcome, one thing is sure: the controversy will continue.

COALS FROM THE SEABED
Among the items raised from the seabed are numerous pieces of coal that spilled out of the bunkers when the ship sank. Of all the rescued artifacts, individual lumps of coal are the only ones to have been sold. The money raised helps to fund further salvage efforts.

Steel fitting, weighing two tonnes (2.2 tons) is recovered from the wreck site

METAL FATIGUE
Investigation of the steel used in the hull revealed that the plates and rivets became brittle when exposed to low water temperatures. On the night of the disaster, the water temperature was about 31°F (−0.2°C). In addition, the steel had a high sulfur content, which made it more liable to fracture, and the rivets used were low grade, making them liable to splinter. This explains why the iceberg caused such serious damage to the hull.

TREASURE TROVE
Many of the artifacts retrieved from the seabed were stored in laboratories in France. There they were kept in stable conditions and used to help scientists study the corrosive effects of seawater. Most of the objects have now been restored, although this was a slow and painstaking process.

A NEW DIRECTION
The ship's compass (above) stood on a wooden stand, a large proportion of which was eaten away by teredos (marine worms). Painstaking conservation has restored the stand to something of its former stature.

Objects are washed in fresh water to remove harmful mud and salt

Concretion of spoons and china from the Titanic *wreck site*

FUSED AS ONE
The corrosive effect of the seawater on metal produces rust that cements objects into unlikely combinations called concretions. Here, spoons and a lump of china have become firmly joined. To separate such artifacts, conservators use electrolysis—passing electricity through metal objects in a chemical bath— to slow further corrosion and soften the concretion.

A collection of well-preserved spoons recovered from the seabed

What happened?

Although some eyewitnesses stated that the ship broke in two before it sank, there has always been some doubt about this, as other witnesses claimed that the ship went down in one piece. The discovery of the wreck in two pieces, some 1,970 ft (600 m) apart on the seabed, confirms that the hull did indeed break up.

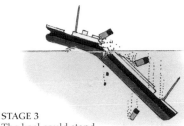

STAGE 1
As the "watertight" compartments filled with water one by one, the bow slowly sank, pulling the stern of the ship upward and out of the water. The angle of the ship began to put great strain on the keel.

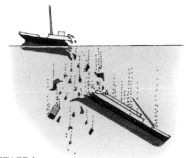

STAGE 3
The keel could stand the strain no more and fractured between the third and fourth funnels. This caused the stern section to right itself and float upright in the water for a few minutes.

STAGE 2
The weight of water inside the hull finally pulled the bow underwater. By now the stern was right up in the air, causing funnels, deck equipment, engines, boilers, and all the internal fittings to break loose and crash forward.

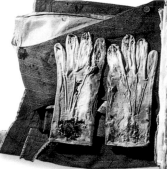

STAGE 4
The bow plummeted forward and downward to the ocean floor. As it did so, it broke free of the stern section, which floated by itself momentarily before it too sank below the waves. Debris was scattered over a wide area of seabed.

SLICED BY ICE
It was long believed that the iceberg sliced into the *Titanic* like a can opener, causing one continuous gash along the hull. The fact that the hull is now buried in up to 55 ft (17 m) of mud made it impossible, until recently, to study the damage. Recent sonar images, however, show that the iceberg actually made six narrow incisions in the ship's hull.

HAND-CLEAN ONLY
The only way to remove the dirt from sea-damaged clothes and restore them to their former glory is by hand. With careful brushing and the use of sensitive cleaning agents and preserving chemicals, the effects of almost 100 years under the sea can slowly be reversed.

Clothes dusted to remove specks of dust and debris

Items of clothing after restoration

GOOD AS NEW
Many items of clothing from the wreck are remarkably well preserved, having survived wrapped up in trunks and suitcases, or folded neatly in drawers. Clothes recovered include a pair of gloves, a neatly pressed shirt, and a steward's jacket.

Rubber gloves protect hands against the harmful effects of chemicals

ONCE THEY SAID GOD HIMSELF COULDN'T SINK HER
NOW THEY SAY NO MAN ON EARTH COULD RAISE HER.

RAISE THE TITANIC

LORD GRADE presents A MARTIN STARGER PRODUCTION
JASON ROBARDS RICHARD JORDAN DAVID SELBY ANNE ARCHER
ALEC GUINNESS
RAISE THE TITANIC
Produced by WILLIAM FRYE Directed by JERRY JAMESON Screenplay by ADAM KENNEDY
Adaptation by ERIC HUGHES From the Novel by CLIVE CUSSLER Music by JOHN BARRY

A DROP IN THE OCEAN
One of the less successful attempts to film the *Titanic* story was *Raise the Titanic* (1980). The film cost many millions to produce and made so little money that the film's producer, Lord Grade, remarked, "It would have been cheaper to lower the Atlantic."

Never-ending story

THE *TITANIC* HAS HAD TWO LIVES. Its first life was as an ill-fated ship that floated for less than a year. Its second life began the moment the ship struck the iceberg and, almost 100 years later, shows no sign of ending. With countless films, books, musicals, songs, computer games, and websites to its name, the *Titanic* is now more famous than ever. Phrases associated with the ship—"tip of the iceberg," "rearranging the deckchairs on the *Titanic*," "and the band played on"—have all entered the English language, and there can be few people who do not have some knowledge of this fascinating story. Even those who have no interest in ships or the sea have been touched by the tragic tale of the *Titanic* and the shocking waste of lives. The *Titanic* may lie rusting at the bottom of the Atlantic, but interest in the ship—and the magical era it was a part of—lives on.

Memorial edition of the Daily Graphic, *April 20, 1912*

Daily Mirror, 16 April 1912

Supplement to the Sphere *Magazine, April 27, 1912*

THE WRECK of the
The Story Told by "Sphere"
Special Twelve-page Sup

S   O

C   Q

THE DAILY-G

The Daily Mirror

DISASTER TO THE TITANIC. WORLD'S LARGEST LINER SINKS AFTER COLLIDING WITH AN ICEBERG DURING HER MAIDEN VOYAGE.

THE
WRECK
of the TITANIC
Descriptive Musical Sketch for the Piano
HAYDON AUGARDE

THE DEATHLESS STORY
OF THE
TITANIC

THE ENTIRE PUBLISHING PROFITS of the first 10,000 Copies have been devoted to the Relief Fund.

NO 172
WITH TONIC SOL-FA.

THE SHIP THAT WILL
NEVER RETURN
(The Loss of the "Titanic.")
SONG
AND
POEM
F. V. ST. CLAIR.

Sheet music for The Wreck of the Titanic, *written by Haydon Augarde*

The Deathless Story of the Titanic, *issued by Lloyds Weekly News, 1912*

Sheet music for The Ship That Will Never Return, *written by F. V. St. Clair*

SILENT STAR
One of the few survivors of the *Titanic* to prosper from the tragedy was the actress Dorothy Gibson, who was traveling first-class and escaped in one of the lifeboats. One month after the ship sank, she co-wrote and starred in a silent movie, *Saved from the Titanic* and went on to have a successful film career. The film was the first of many about the ship.

IN PRINT
Within days of the disaster, newspapers were producing memorial editions packed with photographs and artistic reconstructions of the final tragic hours of the *Titanic*. Songwriters produced mournful songs, postcard companies printed memorial cards with pictures of the ship and its captain, and publishers produced hastily written books.

Kenneth More as Second Officer Lightoller

A NIGHT TO REMEMBER

The publication, in 1955, of Walter Lord's authoritative book *A Night To Remember* sparked renewed interest in the *Titanic*. Lord's interviews with more than 60 survivors brought to life the final hours of those on board the liner. The book was televised in 1956 and, in 1958, was turned into a successful documentary-style film starring Kenneth More.

3-D RECONSTRUCTION

The appeal of the *Titanic* continues into the computer age. Safe in your own home, you can wander around the ship, explore the public rooms and cabins, stand on the deck, and relive the final moments on a 3-D video game.

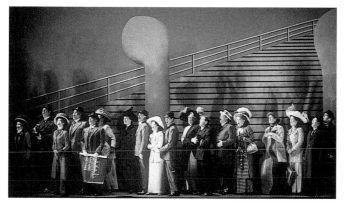

TITANIC MUSICALS

The sinking of the *Titanic* may seem an unlikely subject for a musical, but the larger-than-life character of Molly Brown (p. 40) provided the perfect excuse. *The Unsinkable Molly Brown* opened on Broadway, New York, in 1960 and was a great success. Another musical, *Titanic* (above), staged in 1997 to mark the 85th anniversary of the disaster, highlighted the great divide between the wealthy passengers in first class and the poor immigrants in third class.

Kate Winslet and Leonardo DiCaprio star in the film Titanic *(1997)*

THE BIG TIME

Interest in the *Titanic* reached huge proportions with the release of the film *Titanic* in 1997. Directed by James Cameron and starring Kate Winslet and Leonardo DiCaprio, the film won 11 Oscars, including best picture and best director. Within two years, it had taken $1,826 million at the box office, making it one of the most successful films of all time.

RAISE THE TITANIC?

Ever since the ship sank in 1912, plans have been put forward to raise the ship off the seabed. Relatives of some of the wealthy deceased considered salvaging the ship within days of its sinking. Others proposed attaching magnets or bags of helium to the ship's hull. There was even a scheme to fill the ship with ping-pong balls! As the debate over whether to raise the *Titanic* or leave it in peace continues, the rusting wreck continues to disintegrate.

Did you know?

AMAZING FACTS

Loading coal at the docks

⚑ The *Titanic* was carrying 6,598 tons (5,986 metric tons) of coal to New York.

⚑ Chief Baker Charles Joughin had an amazing escape. He was standing on the stern when it slowly sank into the water and was able to step into the water without even getting his hair wet. He survived in the freezing water for two hours. He was not able to climb onto the upturned collapsible lifeboat B but eventually survivors managed to pull him into lifeboat 12.

⚑ Tins of crackers and water were stowed away in the lifeboats, but the survivors did not know they were there and most did not discover them.

⚑ There were at least nine dogs on board as well as two roosters and two hens. Two of the dogs survived.

Harland and Wolff workmen tightening bolts

⚑ The Harland and Wolff shipyard employed over 15,000 workmen to build the *Olympic* and the *Titanic*. They worked five and a half days a week and, aside from Christmas and Easter, had only a week´s vacation a year.

⚑ The cheapest third-class fare on the *Titanic* was £7 15 shillings, including meals. This was about $40 in 1912, or about $300 today. The most expensive tickets of all were for the promenade suites on B deck and cost £870—about $50,000 today.

⚑ The *Titanic* was transporting goods across the Atlantic. Twelve cases of ostrich plumes were among the cargo.

⚑ Doctors wanted to amputate Richard Norris Williams' legs when he was rescued from the *Titanic*, but he refused to allow it. He recovered fully and went on to win tennis tournaments. He was an Olympic gold medalist in 1924.

Richard Norris Williams

⚑ A daily newspaper, called the *Atlantic Daily Bulletin*, was produced on board the *Titanic*.

⚑ You can smell icebergs before you see them! The minerals in the ice give off a distinctive smell as the icebergs drift southward and melt.

⚑ There were only two bathtubs for more than 700 third-class passengers.

⚑ There was a small hole in the bottom of each lifeboat, to ensure that water did not collect in the boat while it was on deck. Lifeboat 5 had reached the water before its hole was blocked.

⚑ Steam from the *Titanic*'s boilers powered the electricity generator, and about 200 miles (322 km) of electric cable connected it to the lights, machinery, and heating systems. Engineers in the boiler rooms succeeded in keeping the lights working on the *Titanic* until two minutes before it sank.

Ostrich feather

⚑ There was a 50-phone switchboard on the *Titanic*. The crew was able to talk to each other, and some of the first-class rooms had phones, but it was not possible to speak to people on land.

⚑ The original plans allowed room for 64 lifeboats. However, the owners and builders of the *Titanic* reduced the number to 16 in order to provide more space for passengers on the boat deck. They added four lifeboats with collapsible sides.

QUESTIONS AND ANSWERS

Q Why were third-class passengers given a medical check upon boarding?

A Most of the third-class passengers were immigrating and underwent a medical check to make sure they were healthy enough to enter the United States.

Q What are growlers?

A Slabs of ice that have broken away from icebergs or the ice pack are known as growlers. They are often dark in color with little showing above the water line.

Q What were the *Titanic*'s two masts used for?

A A derrick (simple crane) on the foremast lifted cars and other heavy goods in and out of the forehold. A ladder inside the foremast led up to the crow's nest. Wires stretched between the two masts were an important part of the wireless communication system.

Q How many lifeboats are there on ships today?

A Modern cruise ships have enough lifeboats for 25 percent more people than they should have on board.

Q When they found the *Titanic*'s hull, what did explorers see on the foremast?

A The foremast had collapsed across the deck and the crow's nest could still be seen.

There is no smoke from the fourth funnel

The bow of the *Titanic* on the seabed

Q What happened to sick people on the *Titanic*?

A A small hospital with two doctors looked after those who were unwell.

Q Why did the *Titanic* have four funnels?

A The *Titanic*'s owners thought that four funnels would look more impressive than three. The dummy funnel served as a ventilator.

Q Why didn't the lookouts use binoculars?

A Lookouts Frederick Fleet and Reginald Lee thought the binoculars had been left behind in Southampton.

Q Why was the *Titanic*'s maiden voyage delayed from March 20, 1912, to April 10, 1912?

A When the *Olympic* collided with *HMS Hawke* in September 1911, the Harland and Wolff workers had to stop work on the *Titanic* to repair the 40-foot (12-meter) hole in *Olympic*'s side.

Record Breakers

⚓ In 1912, the *Titanic* was the largest ship ever built. Its length of (882 ft 9 in) (269 m) and width of 92 ft 6 in (28 m) were the same as the *Olympic*, but the *Titanic* was slightly heavier.

⚓ At its launch it was claimed that the *Titanic* was the largest man-made object that had been moved.

⚓ To build the *Olympic* and the *Titanic*, Harland and Wolff constructed a huge metal framework, called a gantry. It was the largest gantry in the world.

⚓ The two parlor suites with private promenade decks on B deck were the most beautifully decorated staterooms on any ocean liner.

The White Star Line's New Triple-screw Steamers
"OLYMPIC" ☆ "TITANIC"
LARGEST AND FINEST IN THE WORLD
(SEE OVER)

A contemporary postcard comparing the *Titanic* to the world's tallest buildings

Timeline

THE BUILDING OF THE RMS *TITANIC* and her tragic loss is a story that has fascinated thousands of people over the last century. This timeline sets out the key points, from the transatlantic liner's conception as an idea, through its design, construction, and launch to the fatal collision with the iceberg, the sinking, and finally, many decades later, the discovery of the wreck. The story continues today, with more trips down to the wreck and the raising and restoration of further *Titanic* items.

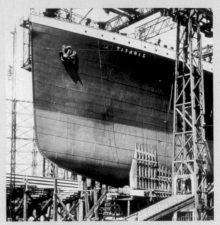

The construction of the *Titanic*

Two of the *Titanic*'s huge propellers

- **SUMMER 1907** Lord Pirrie, chairman of Harland and Wolff Shipbuilders, and Bruce Ismay, director of the White Star Line, decide to build three huge, luxurious liners called *Olympic*, *Titanic*, and *Britannic*.

- **MARCH 31, 1909** Construction of the *Titanic* begins.

- **MAY 31, 1911** *Titanic* is launched, watched by more than 100,000 people.

- **MARCH 31, 1912** Fitting out is complete and the *Titanic* is ready to sail.

- **APRIL 2, 1912** Tugs pull the *Titanic* out to sea for her sea trials. **8:00 p.m.** The *Titanic* leaves Belfast for Southampton.

- **APRIL 3, 1912** Shortly before midnight the *Titanic* arrives in Southampton having traveled 570 miles (917 km).

- **APRIL 4–10, 1912** Last-minute painting and the fitting of furniture and carpets; the hiring of the seamen, firemen, and stewards; loading coal into the bunkers, cargo into the holds, and provisions for the journey.

- **APRIL 5, 1912** Flags and pennants adorn the ship to salute the people of Southampton and mark Good Friday.

- **WEDNESDAY, APRIL 10, 1912** **6:00 a.m.** Crew boards *Titanic*. **6:30 a.m.** Thomas Andrews arrives. **7:30 a.m.** Captain Smith boards. **9:30 a.m.** Bruce Ismay arrives. He will stay in one of the parlor suites with a private promenade deck.

Third-class daily menu

9:30–11:30 a.m. Passengers board. At **12:00 noon** *Titanic* finally sets sail for France, but is slightly delayed by the near collision with the *New York*. **6:35 p.m.** *Titanic* drops anchor in Cherbourg harbor. Two small White Star steamships bring passengers, luggage ,and mail out to the *Titanic*. **8:10 p.m.** *Titanic* sets off for Ireland.

- **THURSDAY, APRIL 11** **11:30 a.m.** *Titanic* arrives at Queenstown and anchors 2 miles (3 km) off shore. **1:30 p.m.** *Titanic* leaves Queenstown and sets sail for New York.

- **FRIDAY, APRIL 12** *Titanic* receives wireless messages of congratulations on the maiden voyage, and also warning that there is ice in the sea lanes. Captain Smith steers farther south.

- **SATURDAY, APRIL 13** **11:00 p.m.** The wireless machine stops working. Jack Phillips and his assistant Harold Bride work all night and repair it by 5:00 a.m.

Titanic leaves Queenstown (now known as Cobh)

• SUNDAY, APRIL 14

9:00 a.m. *Titanic* receives an ice warning from the *Caronia*. Captain Smith sends it to the officers on the bridge.

11:40 a.m. Dutch liner *Noordam* reports that there is a lot of ice.

1:42 p.m. White Star Liner *Baltic* warns of icebergs and field ice. Captain Smith shows this warning to Bruce Ismay.

1:45 p.m. German liner *Amerika* reports two large icebergs. This message fails to reach Captain Smith.

Harold Bride at work in the radio room

7:30 p.m. Harold Bride overhears an ice warning from the *Californian* and sends it to the bridge. The ice is approximately 50 miles (80 km) ahead.

9:30 p.m. Second Officer Lightoller instructs the lookouts to "keep a sharp lookout for ice."

9:30 p.m. The steamer *Mesaba* warns of pack ice and large icebergs. Jack Phillips is busy sending passengers' messages and

Lifeboats row away as the stern sinks

does not send the warning to the bridge.

10:55 p.m. Jack Phillips, exhausted, cuts off the *Californian's* ice warning.

11:40 p.m. Lookout Frederick Fleet sees the iceberg. First Officer Murdoch orders the engine room to stop the engines and put them in reverse, tells Quartermaster Robert Hichens, who is at the wheel, to turn "hard a'starboard" (sharp left) and closes the doors between the watertight compartments.

11:40 p.m. The *Titanic* hits the iceberg, only 37 seconds after Fleet's warning.

11:41 p.m. Captain Smith instructs Fourth Officer Boxhall to inspect the ship for damage.

11:50 p.m. Thomas Andrews inspects the damaged areas.

• MONDAY, APRIL 15

12:00 midnight Thomas Andrews tells Captain Smith the ship will sink within an hour and a half.

12:05 a.m. Captain Smith orders the lifeboats to be uncovered.

12:10 a.m. Captain Smith asks Jack Phillips to send out a call for help. He uses the Morse code distress signal, "CQD." Later he uses the new international call, "SOS." The *Olympic, Frankfurt,* and *Carpathia* reply.

12:25 a.m. *Carpathia* sets off to the rescue, but is 58 miles (93 km) away.

12:45 a.m. The first lifeboat is lowered.

12:45 a.m. The first distress flare is fired.

About **1:00 a.m.** First news reaches the US that the *Titanic* has struck an iceberg.

2:05 a.m. The last lifeboat is lowered.

2:17 a.m. The bow plunges under the water.

2:18 a.m. The *Titanic* breaks into two. The bow section sinks.

2:20 a.m. Two of the collapsible lifeboats wash overboard, one half-flooded, the other upside down.

2:20 a.m. The stern sinks.

4:10 a.m. Survivors from the first lifeboat board *Carpathia*.

8.10 a.m. Survivors from the last lifeboat board *Carpathia*.

12:00 a.m. Reports reach New York that the *Titanic* is still afloat and all are safe.

6:16 p.m. Captain Haddock of the *Olympic*, the *Titanic's* sister ship, confirms that the *Titanic* has sunk.

• TUESDAY, APRIL 16

Carpathia sends a list of survivors, which is posted outside the *New York Times* office.

The Titanic's propellers rise out of the water

• WEDNESDAY, APRIL 17

The *Mackay-Bennett*, a small steamer chartered by the White Star Line, leaves Halifax. It searches the area for nine days and finds 306 bodies. Later steamers find another 22 bodies.

• THURSDAY, APRIL 18

Carpathia reaches New York with 705 survivors.

• APRIL 19—MAY 25

Inquiry into the disaster by the US Senate.

• MAY 2—JULY 3

British Board of Trade Inquiry into the disaster.

• MAY 14

Dorothy Gibson, one of the survivors, writes and stars in a silent movie *Saved from the Titanic*.

Survivors reach the *Carpathia*

• JULY 3, 1958

World Premiere of the film *A Night To Remember*.

• 1960

Opening of the musical *The Unsinkable Molly Brown*.

• JULY 1980, JUNE 1981, JULY 1983

American Jack Grimm leads three attempts to find the wreck.

• SEPTEMBER 1, 1985

Robert Ballard's French/American expedition with search ship *Knorr* and uncrewed submersible *Argo* discovers the wreck of the *Titanic*.

• JULY 1986

Robert Ballard returns and photographs the wreck in a tiny submarine called *Alvin*.

• JULY 1987

A salvaging expedition, with search ship *Nadir* and crewed submersible *Nautile* starts lifting objects from the wreck. Further expeditions in 1993 and 1994 raise more than 5,000 objects.

• 1991

A Soviet/Canadian expedition films the wreck for a documentary called *Titanica*.

• DEC 18, 1997

The film *Titanic* opens in the US.

• APRIL 2003

Premiere of the film *Ghosts of the Abyss*.

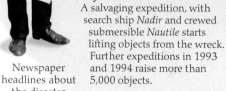

Newspaper headlines about the disaster

The crewed submersible *Nautile*

Find out more

OLYMPIC STORY
The sister ships *Titanic* and *Olympic* were so similar that by finding out more about the *Olympic*, you will learn a great deal about the design and style of the *Titanic*.

IF THE STORY OF THE *TITANIC* has captured your imagination, there are many ways to find out more. You can visit one of the memorials to the *Titanic* and her crew. There are a number of permanent exhibitions about the *Titanic* and frequent special exhibitions, which often show objects that have been raised from the wreck. By looking at the plans or making a model, you will learn a great deal, while watching one of the films about the *Titanic* will bring the liner's tragic last journey to life.

THE GRAND STAIRCASE
There are a number of permanent exhibitions about the *Titanic*, but you will also find that there are excellent temporary exhibitions to attend. Organizers do all they can to recreate the atmosphere on board the luxurious liner and to give an idea of the different experiences of first-class, second-class, and third-class passengers. The ornate grand staircase, under an elaborate glass dome, was one of the most striking parts of the *Titanic*'s first-class accommodations.

USEFUL WEBSITES

- To find out about the Titanic Historical Society, see: **www. titanichistoricalsociety.org/index.asp**
- For all kinds of information about the *Titanic*, go to: **www.titanic-titanic.com**
- To find out about individual passengers and crew members, see: **www.encyclopedia-titanica.org/**
- For a transcript of the US Senate and British Board of Trade inquiry, go to: **www.titanicinquiry.org/**
- For information about Molly Brown, and the Molly Brown House Museum in the US, see: **http://mollybrown.org**
- To visit an online community dedicated to sharing facts and images relating to the *Titanic*, go to: **www.titanic.com**

The Belfast Titanic *memorial was unveiled on June 26, 1920*

REMEMBERING THE DEAD
There are many memorials in different parts of the world dedicated to people or groups of people lost on the *Titanic*. In Southampton, England, there are separate memorials to the engineers, firemen, musicians, and postmen who worked on the *Titanic*. In Belfast, Northern Ireland, there is a memorial dedicated to the 22 men from Ulster who died in the disaster.

A *TITANIC* MODEL

Constructing a model of the *Titanic* will help you understand its incredible size. You will find out about the boat deck and exactly where all the lifeboats were kept. You will also understand how frightening it was for the people in the first lifeboats as they were lowered about 60 ft (18 m) from the boat deck down to the water.

Deck plans for the White Star Line Triple-Screw Royal Mail Steamship Titanic

PLANS FOR THE DECKS

If you study the detailed plans for each deck of the *Titanic* you can discover interesting details such as where the vegetables were kept, which deck housed the squash courts, and where to find the passage known as "Scotland Road."

GHOSTS OF THE ABYSS

If you want to find out more about the *Titanic* wreck, you need to see the 2003 film *Ghosts of the Abyss*, by James Cameron, director of *Titanic*. Using digital 3-D technology it takes you on an amazing expedition down to the seabed for a trip around the wreck. To find out more about the passengers and crew and to see fantastic recreations of the *Titanic's* interior, watch the films *A Night To Remember* (1958) and *Titanic* (1997).

This part of the liner was below the water line

Places to visit

THE MARINER'S MUSEUM, NEWPORT NEWS, VIRGINIA

The displays of oceangoing commercial steamships, in the Great Hall of Steam Gallery, include an exhibition on the *Titanic*.

THE MARITIME MUSEUM, FALL RIVER, MASSACHUSETTS

The museum's collection includes photographs, the account of a *Titanic* survivor, a video of the underwater discovery, and the certerpiece, a 28-foot (8.5 meter) model of the RMS *Titanic*.

THE TITANIC MEMORIAL LIGHTHOUSE, NEW YORK, NEW YORK

The lighthouse stands 60 feet (18.3 m) tall at the entrance of the South Street Seaport in Manhattan. It holds a light that stands as a tribute to the people who died on the *Titanic*. The Memorial Light originally stood at the old Seaman's Church Insitute, where it signaled to ships in the harbor. The memorial has been a fixture at the Seaport since 1976.

MARITIME MUSEUM OF THE ATLANTIC, HALIFAX, CANADA

The exhibition explores the response of Halifax to the sinking of the *Titanic*. It features artifacts pulled from the water within weeks of the tragedy, including a deck chair, part of the grand staircase, and some carved oak paneling. The exhibition traces the creation of this luxurious "floating palace."

THE TITANIC MUSEUM, INDIAN ORCHARD, MASSACHUSETTS

Edward S. Kamuda founded this private museum in 1963 for the survivors of the ship. It contains a unique collection of personal items from survivors, such as letters, postcards, inspection cards, and menus. It sells models of the *Titanic*, posters, and photographs.

Medal given to the crew of the Carpathia

SALVAGE EXPEDITIONS

Over the years since the *Titanic* was found, salvagers have raised thousands of objects from the wreck and the debris field. Here a robotic arm is lifting a mast-head lamp. Many of the items raised and conserved, such as pieces of White Star china, a piccolo in its case, or a silver matchbox, later feature in touring exhibitions. It is worth seeking out these collections in order to build up a more complete picture of life on board the *Titanic*.

Glossary

AFT Toward or at the rear of a ship.

AFT DECK An open deck toward the back of the ship for use by third-class passengers.

BEDROOM STEWARD(ESS) A person who serves tea, makes beds, and cleans staterooms and lounges.

BERTH A bed or bunk in a cabin.

BOAT DECK The deck on which the lifeboats are stored.

BOILER A closed container that heats water to supply steam or heat.

BOW The front part of the ship.

BRIDGE The control center of the ship.

BULKHEAD The cross-wall in the hold of a ship that can create a watertight compartment.

CABIN An office or living room on a ship.

CLIPPER SHIP A fast sailing ship.

COLLAPSIBLE A lifeboat with canvas sides that collapse for easy storage. There were four collapsible lifeboats on the *Titanic*.

CQD An international Morse code distress call that was later replaced by SOS.

CREW The people who run a ship. There were 898 on the *Titanic*'s crew list: 875 men and 23 women.

A. M. Carlisle, designer of the *Titanic*, at the British investigation

CROW'S NEST A lookout platform high on a ship's mast. On the *Titanic* the crow's-nest was 90 ft (27 m) above the water.

DAVIT One of a pair of cranelike devices equipped with pulleys and ropes and used to lower lifeboats.

DRY DOCK A dock that can be pumped dry for work on the bottom of a ship.

ENGINEER A person who helps run the engines and machines.

ENSIGN A flag distinguishing a country or company.

FIREMAN A person who loads coal into the ship's boilers.

FITTING OUT Installing the decks, machinery, and other equipment inside the empty hull.

FUNNEL A tall chimney through which smoke from the engines can escape.

FURNACES An enclosed chamber in which coal burns to produce heat. There were 159 furnaces in 29 boilers on the *Titanic*.

GALLEY STAFF The people who work in the ship's kitchen.

The 1958 film *A Night To Remember*

GANGWAY A passageway into a ship.

GENERAL ROOM A public room like a lounge for the third-class passengers.

GRAND STAIRCASE The staircase connecting the first-class dining room with the first-class promenade deck.

GREASER A person who attends to a ship's engines.

A washbasin raised from the wreck

GROSS REGISTERED TONNAGE (GRT) The total internal volume of a ship.

HOLD The space in a ship below decks for storing cargo.

HULL The main body of a ship.

ICE FIELD A large area of ice in the ocean.

INSPECTION CARD Carried by immigrants, the inspection card states the person's name, former country of residence, port of departure, and vessel for the journey.

KEEL The bottom structure that runs the length of a ship in the very center and to which the frames fasten.

LINER A large passenger ship that sails fixed routes ("lines").

LOOKOUTS The *Titanic* had six lookouts. Working in pairs they kept watch for other ships or obstacles ahead from the crow's nest on the foremast.

A reconstruction of the first-class veranda café on the *Titanic*

LOWER DECK This is the deck above the orlop deck. On the *Titanic* it was just above the waterline.

MAIDEN VOYAGE A ship's first journey.

MORSE CODE A telegraph code used to send messages. A system of dots and dashes represents letters and numbers.

MUSICIANS There were eight musicians working on the *Titanic*. A quintet held concerts for the first-class passengers, while a trio played in the reception room by the à la carte restaurant.

ORLOP DECK The lowest deck.

PASSAGEWAY A walkway between cabins or other rooms.

POOP DECK A raised deck at the stern of a ship.

PORT The left-hand side of a ship.

PORTHOLE A small, usually round, window in the side of a ship. There were about 2,000 portholes and windows on the *Titanic*.

PROMENADE DECK An upper deck that was sometimes enclosed, where people could take a walk.

PROPELLERS Three large propellers, driven by the engine, moved the *Titanic* through the water.

QUARTERMASTER A junior officer with particular responsibility for navigation.

QUOITS A game that involved tossing rings at a stake on the deck.

RIVETS A short metal pin used to fasten things together.

READING ROOM A spacious, quiet room used by women in particular for reading and writing.

RECIPROCATING STEAM ENGINE A steam engine in which a piston moves backward and forward inside a cylinder.

ROYAL MAIL SHIP (RMS) A ship with a contract to carry mail from one place to another. The *Titanic* was carrying 3,364 sacks of mail.

RUDDER A vertical fin at the back of a ship, used for steering. The *Titanic*'s rudder was taller than a five-story building.

SALOON A large, public room on a ship. The first-class dining room was also called the dining saloon and was the largest room on the *Titanic*. It could seat 550 people.

SEAMAN A person who helps with the day-to-day running of a ship.

A doll rescued from the *Titanic*

SEA TRIALS Tests conducted at sea on a new ship to make sure the engines and steering are working well.

SHIPPING LINE A company that owns and runs passenger or freight ships.

SISTER SHIP One that is the same class and belongs to the same line.

SMOKING ROOM A room where men could smoke; the *Titanic* had three.

SOS Morse code distress call. The *Titanic* was one of the first ships to use this code. The earlier distress call was CQD.

STARBOARD The right-hand side of a ship.

STATEROOM A first-class private cabin.

STEAM TURBINE A machine that takes the energy of steam and turns it into the movement of a bladed propeller.

STEERAGE The cheapest accommodation on a passenger ship.

STERN The rear part of a ship.

STEWARD(ESS) A person who sets the tables, serves food, and clears tables in the dining rooms.

STOKER A person who looks after the furnaces on a steamship.

SUBMERSIBLE A submarine designed and equipped to carry out work deep on the seabed.

One of *Titanic*'s lifeboats

TRIMMER A person who wheels coal to the boilers and ensures that the remaining fuel is evenly distributed so that the ship is balanced.

TURKISH BATH A steam bath, for the use of first-class passengers.

WHEELHOUSE The enclosed structure on the bridge of a ship where officers steer the vessel.

WIRELESS OPERATORS The two people, employed by Marconi, who sent Morse code telegraph messages.

The *Titanic*'s bow on the seabed

Looking shipshape: model of the *Titanic*

Lifeboats are launched—
from the 1997 film *Titanic*

Index

Acknowledgments

Dorling Kindersley would like to thank:
Richard Chasemore for *Titanic* illustration (pp. 12–16)
Illustrators: John Woodcock, Hans Jenssen
Indexer: Chris Bernstein
Researcher: Robert Graham
Editorial assistance: Carey Scott

For this edition, the publisher would also like to thank: Lisa Stock for editorial assistance; David Ekholm-JAlbum, Sunita Gahir, Susan Reuben, Susan St Louis, Lisa Stock, & Bulent Yusuf for the clip art; Sue Nicholson & Edward Kinsey for the wall chart; Monica Byles & Stewart J Wild for proofreading; Margaret Parrish & John Searcy for Americanization.

Picture credits:
The publisher would like to thank the following for their kind permission to reproduce their photographs:

(Key: a-above; b-below/bottom; c-center; f-far; l-left; r-right; t-top)

Alamy Images: Dinodia Photo Library 62-63 bckgrd; Popperfoto 67tl. **AKG London:** 19br, 23 tr, 37bl, 40- 41, 44b. **Howard Barlow:** 53br. **Bridgeman Art Library, London / New York:** © Harley Crossley 38-39; V & A Museum, London 8tr. **British Sailors' Society:** 4r, 34c. **Christie's Images Ltd 1999:** 43tl. **Colorific:** 19tl, 57cr; P. Landmann / Arenok 4br, 5tr, 5br, 5tl, 6br, 6tl, 6tr, 19cr, 29tl, 30bl, 56br, 56tr, 57bl; RMS Titanic / Arenok 56cl. **Corbis UK Ltd:** 9br, 11br, 18tr, 25tr, 34bl, 38l, 39tc, 47c, 48br, 51tr, 52-53, 54bl, 54br, 57tl, 12bl, 62cl; Bettmann 11tr, 64bl, 67tr; Bettmann / UPI 42tl, 58bl; The Mariners Museum, Virginia 17tr, 65cl; Christie's Images 64tl; Hulton-Deutsch Collection 64tr; Polak Matthew 65bl; Rien / Sygma 67br; Geray Sweeney 64bl; Ralph White 61br, 62tr, 65b. **Cyberflix:** 20tl, 21tr, 59tr. **DK Images:** Judith Miller and Cobwebs of Southampton 70tr; Southampton City Cultural Services 65clb. **E.T. Archive:** Denis Cochrane Collection 6cr, 48tl. **Frank Spooner Pictures:** 36bl, 55br; Jahiel/ Liaison/ Gamma, 26tr, 55bl, 56bc; Liaison/ Gamma 40t. **Getty Images:** Merie Wallace / AFP 68-69. **Harland & Wolff Photographic Collection:** 10-11, 11cr, 11tl, 12tr, 12br, 13tl, 22br, 29br. **Hulton Getty:** 13br, 18bl, 28cl, 28c, 35tr, 38bl, 41tl, 43tr, 45tr, 46br, 49bl, 50r, 51l. **Illustrated London News Picture Library:** 37br, 50b. **The Irish Picture Library:** © Father S. J. Brown Collection 20br. **John Frost Newspapers:** 47bl, 47tr. **Kobal Collection:** 20th C. Fox / Paramount 32tl; Merie W. Wallace 24c. **Courtesy of James & Felicia Kreuzer:** 32cl. **Stanley Lehrer:** 20cr, 23cr, 45br. **Paul Louden-Brown Collection:** 10l, 27tr, 52cl. **Joe Low:** 24tl, 42-43. **Joan Marcus:** 59tr. **Courtesy of The Mariner's Museum, Newport News VA:** 36tr, 38tr, 43cr, 45tl. **Photographed by Learning Resources Technology,** courtesy of the Maritime Museum of the Atlantic, Halifax, Nova Scotia, Canada: 37bc. **Mary Evans Picture Library:** 6bl, 9bc, 15tr, 23tl, 24-25, 25cl, 26-27, 26tl, 26tc, 27cr, 32bl, 34-35, 37tr, 41tr, 42tr, 42, 44r, 45bl, 48cl, 49tl, 49tr. **National Maritime Museum, London:** 5bl, 9tr, 13tr, 20cr, 21bl, 23br, 29cl, 35br, 39cr, 50tl, 54-55. **© National Museums and Galleries of Northern Ireland, Ulster Folk and Transport Museum:** 13bl. **National Museums and Galleries on Merseyside:** 4, 23c, 65tc. **Onslow's Titanic Picture Library:** 7, 14tl, 19cl, 21br, 21tl, 27br, 28b, 29bl, 30cl, 32br, 49cr. **The Picture Desk:** The Art Archive / Ocean Memorabilia Collection 63cl, 63tl, 65tr, 66-67 bckgrd. **Popperfoto:** 18-19, 30tl, 51b; Onslow's 28r, 58r. **Quadrant Picture Library:** Mike Nicholson 51cr. **Rex Features:** 10tr, 34tl, 34tr, 36br, 40l, 59bl; Charles Sachs 19tr; Nils Jorgansen 6cl, 16t; Sipa 44tl; Sipa (Cork Examiner) 31tl; Peter Brooker 64tr, 64-65 bckgrd, 66bl. **Ronald Grant Archive:** 58tl, 59tl. **Science & Society Picture Library:** 8b, 8cr. **Southampton City Cultural Services:** 21c, 23bl, 47br, 63tr, 63c, 66tc. **Still Pictures:** B & C Alexander 22cl; Vincent Bretagnolle 33b. **Sygma / RMS Titanic Inc.:** 55tl, 55cra, Bourseiller 28tl; Sotheby's 48cr. **The Titanic Historical Society Collection:** 4tr, 26bl, 27tl, 30-31b, 31cl, 33tl, 41cr, 46tl, 48tr, 52tr; Courtesy Mrs Ruth Becker Blanchard 44cl; Goldsmith 31tr; Ken Marschall 53c. **Courtesy of © "Titanic Survivor"** by Violet Jessop edited by John Maxtone-Graham – Sheridan House Inc. – 1997: 53tr. **Topham Picturepoint:** 18tr, 20bl, 22bl, 29tr, 33tr, 35tc, 36tl, 39tl, 46c, 49br; Buena Vista Pictures 65cb; PressNet 62c; UPPA Ltd 63br, 66cr. **Vintage Magazine Company Ltd:** 31cr. **Louis Vuitton, Paris:** 24cl. **Stuart Williamson:** 53tl, 59br.

Wall chart
DK Images: National Maritime Museums Liverpool (Merseyside Maritime Museum) c; Rough Guides cl (Titanic interior); **Getty Images:** Topical Press Agency / Hulton Archive bl; **PA Photos:** Ralph White / AP br.

Jacket
Front: Bettmann/Corbis, b; The Titanic Sinking on 15th April 1912, 1991, by Harley Crossley/ Private Collection/www.bridgeman.co.uk, tc; Mary Evans Picture Library, tr. Back: The Art Archive: Ocean Memorabilia Collection, bc; DK Picture Library:Southampton City Cultural Services, br; Corbis: Ralph White, tr; Katz/FSP, cr; Rex Features, l; Stanley Lehrer, cbl.

All other images
© Dorling Kindersley
For further information see:
www.dkimages.com